A HuLlaBaLoO At tHe LoCaL ZoO

MaRk RoLaNd LaNgDaLe

Pen Press

First published in Great Britain by Pen Press

All paper used in the printing of this book has been made from wood grown in managed, sustainable forests.

ISBN13: 978-1-78003-104-0

Printed and bound in the UK
Pen Press is an imprint of Indepenpress Publishing Limited
25 Eastern Place
Brighton
BN2 1GJ

A catalogue record of this book is available from
the British Library

Cover design by Jacqueline Abromeit

Big ups to - my mum & dad, Jackie, Lindsey, Neil, Ben, Alex, Fraser, Briony, Iain, Jeff, Jo, Fiona, Mark C, Daphnne, Helena, Mike & Michaela. And my beloved Accrington Stanley.

This book is complete nonsense from beginning to end, in fact this book is more nonsensical than a children's pantomime which isn't a bad line when found in a book of nonsense rhymes.

However there are 19 sensible rhymes in this book athough you might well find there's a fine line between what's sensible and what's nonsense, well when you read this book you can make up your own mind.

-*Credo quia absurdum est:* (I believe because it is absurd)

I hope this book encourages you to write your own poems stories and rhymes because when all's said and done words should be fun!

CoNtEntS

ELePhAntS LoVe tO DiScO DaNcE
(ThE TrUnKaTeD VeRsiOn)

Elephants love to disco dance
Well they would if you gave 'em
Half a chance.

They also like to jump and jive
But if you partnered one
You might not survive.

They like to do the conga too
And sometimes they do the boogaloo
And it tends to create quite a hullabaloo
'Coz when they do they haven't a clue.

Elephants love to disco dance.
They tap and clap and hop and prance.
But be careful they don't step on you by chance!
Yes, elephants love to disco dance!

Excuse me, I said excuse me! we've just received
A trunk call is there an elephant in the room?!!

JiGsAwS ArE A PuZzLe

Jigsaws are a puzzle
They're very hard to do
But believe you me
They're even harder if you're a kangaroo!

ExCuSe tHe PuN!

Excuse the pun
But nothing can eclipse the sight
Of the moon passing across the sun!

TeN LiTtLe ALiEnS StAnDiNg iN A LiNe

Ten little aliens standing in a line
One spontaneously combusted and then there were nine.

Nine little aliens getting ready for a date
One fell down the stairs and then there were eight.

Eight little aliens looking towards the heavens
One got abducted and then there were seven.

Seven little aliens performing guitar licks
One got electrocuted and then there were six.

Six little aliens on Earth had arrived
One choked on a fly and then there were five.

Five little aliens walking through the door
One fell through the floorboards and then there were four.

Four little aliens went for a swim in the sea
One met a shark and then there were three.

Three little aliens visiting the zoo
A lion ate one and then there were two.

Two little aliens toting ray guns
One backfired and then there was one.

One little alien standing on his own so
He phoned E.T. who came and took him home!

ThE ArMcHaiR ReFeReE

Believe you me nothing gets past the armchair referee
Or his two assistant referees and the fourth official
Sitting behind him on the settee eating their tea.

Yes, for the armchair referee it's not hard to give a red card
Without all the players surrounding you and without the
Crowd booing and singing you don't know what you're doing,
You don't know what you're doing!

When you're the armchair referee in charge of the whistle,
It's easy to disallow four perfectly good goals by Partick
Thistle. And I think it's fair to say you'll never have a problem
Keeping up with play and you get all the decisions right,
With the aid of the action replay.

Being the armchair referee you're always in the right spot
And are never wrong in fact you could say with penalties
The armchair referee is always spot on!

And you don't get distracted or miss a single thing,
Least of all when the phone rings,
And as the crowd roars you say under your breath,
'That's what the answer machines for!'

Yes, don't you see nothing gets past the armchair referee?
Why? Because the armchair referee is YOU and ME!!

I ThiNk tHe ReAL IsSuE iS YoU MiGhT NeEd A BiGgEr BoX Of TiSsUeS!

There was a young man from Corfu
Who when sneezing made a hullabaloo
With no word of a lie this word he did cry

Attishyooooooooooo
Attishyoooooooooo
Attishyooooooo!

WhO's tHe DaDdy?

In the insect world as a rule
The crane fly is the daddy of them all!

PriM AnD PrOpEr

In school our teacher Mr. Prim
Is always very proper (as a rule),
Until one day we saw him out doing wheelies
On the pavement on his chopper (how uncool).
And then he came a cropper and was arrested
By a great big copper.
Then Mr. Prim wasn't so prim and proper (after all).
I wonder if next week we'll see him out on his
Space hopper chewing a gobstopper outside
The happy shopper (the silly old fool!)

ThE WoRLd'S GrEaTeSt MaGiCiaN

I just may have to rethink my position
As the world's greatest magician
As the last time I attempted to pull a rabbit out of a
hat It turned out to be a cat!

CaTcHiNg HiPpOpOtOMi

With no word of a lie
Last night while I was asleep I swallowed a Hippopotomi
Don't ask me how or why,
I would have much rather swallowed a fly!
Much to my surprise from the horrified Hippopotomi
(in my stomach)
Came this plaintive cry 'Oh my, oh my I wish you'd swallowed
A fly too, let's hope neither of us die!'
(Still I suppose it could have been worse I could have
Swallowed a humpback whale, that's an even taller tale!)

This rhyme was based on the expression catching flies
Which is when you're asleep and your mouth is open wide.

Apparently while we are asleep every year we will swallow
Three spiders, five flies and one Hippopotomi!

NeVeR LeT A GnU TelL YoU WhAt tO Do

Never let a duck push his luck
Never panda to a salamander.
Never let a stingray get his own way.
Never let a hound push you around.
Never kowtow to an owl.
Never let a cat or a rat, for that matter in fact
give you any back chat.
Never let a kangaroo get one over on you.
Never let a giraffe have the last laugh.
Never let a goose or a moose let loose or pull
the wool over your eyes with some lame excuse.
Never let a hippo steal your lippo.
Never let a crow step on your toes.
Never let a chimpanzee sit on your knee
especially if it's got flees.
Never let a marmoset make a monkey out of you
or get you upset.
Never let a panda get the upper hand know for that
you must never stand.
Never let a shark take you to task or in your glory bask.
Never let a woodchuck start a ruck or pass the buck.
Never let a frog jump the gun if you'll excuse the pun.
And most importantly of all never, never, never, never
let a gnu tell you what to do!

MuSiC tO tHe EaRs (A TeAr tO tHe EyE)

When you hear birds sing and bells ring,
The rustle of leaves in the wind,
A clock chime and words rhyme.
The rhythm of a good marching band
Playing in time.
It's like music to the ears.

And when you watch a whale dive
Or see beauty die
Or a rainbow appears in the sky
Or you hear a mother singing a lullaby,
It can often bring a tear to the eye.

I BoUgHt A VeNuS FlyTrAp

I bought a venus flytrap
Because I thought it was pretty cool
And took it home to my mum and dad
And put it in the hall.
Then it grew and grew, it grew so very tall,
So I had to put it outside up against the garden wall.
Then one day it opened up its trap and ate my pussy cat,
Ate the garden wall, came inside and ate the hall
Ate my baseball cap ate my baby brother Pat,
Even ate my mum and dad the dirty little rat.
I didn't think the venus flytrap was quite so cool
After that so I took it back.
What happened to the venus flytrap after that
Is anyone's guess, but my guess is it probably
Ate someone else's cat and is now laying
On the mat in a dream with a great big smile on its face
Like the venus flytrap that got the cream!

ThE SeArCh FoR E.T.

Where would be the most likely place to find E.T.?

Answer: Down the back of the settee!

S.E.T.I.– The Search for Extra-terrestrial Intelligence

ThE RaPpiNg SpEaKiNg CLoCk

I'm the most precise rapper on the block,
I'm the rapping speaking clock.
I'll tell you the time
And do it in rhyme.
It's one thirty one on the dot!

TriCk Or TrEaT?

A witch's teeth are quite unique,
They're blacker than a wizard's feet.
When out at night they like to speak.
Well, that's the trick now where's the treat?
The treat is you never have to wash a wizard's feet
Or ever have to clean a witch's teeth!
  (Witch must be quite a relief!!)

ThAt'S BaTtY

I knew a little bat
That used to flap and flap
It flapped into a cat flap
It didn't flap after that!

YoU CaN ALwAyS CoUnT On DrAcULa

You can always count on Dracula for a few good
biting remarks.
And as long as you don't mind being maimed or scratched,
I'd have to stick my neck out and say
Dracula is actually a pretty good catch!

SuDOkU

Sudoku you're not hip you're square!

CrEePy CrAwLiEs

Nasty creepy crawlies running across the floor.
I know they're out to get me, of that I'm pretty sure.
Nasty creepy crawlies coming through the door
spiders, daddy-long-legs, insects, bugs galore.
Nasty creepy crawlies hiding in my bed
how I really hate them and wish they all were dead.
Nasty creepy crawlies building up their nests,
how I do detest them, the horrid little pests.
Nasty creepy crawlies spinning in their webs
I really hope they don't fall out and land upon
my head!
Nasty creepy crawlies you better had beware
If I were you I wouldn't.....................
be sleeping there on the stairs!

My DaD tHe WiZaRd

My dad thinks he's a wizard,
He wears a pointy hat.
He hides down in the cellar
With Merlin our black and white cat.

He tries to make up potions
And dabbles in magic spells,
But the only thing that magic spells, is trouble,
When Mum yells 'What's that smell?'

My dad thinks he's a wizard
When making his wizard's brew,
But the only brew that he can make
Involves a tea bag he's left to stew.

He reads his *Harry Potter* books
And pours over every page,
In the hope that one day he'll find a spell
That will reverse his age.

My dad thinks he's a wizard
And I think my mum's a witch,
But the only time that I'm a wizard
Is on the football pitch.

My dad thinks he's a wizard
My friends have often said
So if that's true how come last week
He got locked in the garden shed?!

PoEtRy iS

Poetry is
Painting pictures with words,
Sublime images that rhyme, (or not)
Grasped from the mind and put into verse.
Reading things written that may never be heard.
Setting suns,
Swooping swallows,
A bird on the wire,
Butterflies wings
And other indefinable things.
A moment captured in time
Or perhaps a nonsense rhyme.
For a newborn or for someone you mourn
Or a heart that's been torn
Leaving a lover left forlorn.
Some poetry can make you weep
While other poetry can send you off to sleep
Some poetry you throw away
And some you keep.
Poetry is whatever you want it to be
Try writing some and see.

There's no need to look so poe(faced just)try!

DiSaPpEariNg FaSt

Magic is disappearing fast,
Like the rainforest the gnu and rainbows too

The snow on top of Mt Kilimanjaro
Is disappearing fast,
Like komodo dragons, the coral reef
And shooting stars.

Pavement paintings on a rainy day
Are disappearing fast,
Like the panda the rabbit-eared bandicoot
And ice cream in a heat wave.

Invisible ink is disappearing fast
Like gorillas in the mist,
The great and little bustard and white rhinos too

The invisible man is disappearing fast
Like the polar ice caps,
Siamese crocodiles,
Whales and some dog's tails!

Smoke trails from a jet plane
Are disappearing fast,
Like the ozone layer and the oozealum bird,
No, sorry according to the myth that's already
Disappeared up its own rear!
(Ouch! that must have produced a few tears!!)

A No NoNsEnSe RhYmE

This is a no nonsense rhyme.
It doesn't waste time with pretence,
Never sits on the fence.
Doesn't easily take offence
Or need defence,
For being politically incorrect.
Tries to condense the past and the present tense,
Hence is never to dense with words
That don't make any sense and, best of all,
Costs one pound not ninety nine pence!

(Actually for a no nonsense rhyme that last line
   doesn't make a whole lot of sense!)

ThE GiRL ThAt FeLL DoWn THe WiShiNg WeLL

One day Michelle was sitting on the edge of a wishing well,
When she fell, and as she fell and fell and fell and fell (well it
Was a very deep wishing well!) she started to YELL and
YELL and YELL, until poor old Michelle hit the bottom of the
Wishing well with a splash wishing she hadn't fell!).

And as she did Michelle swallowed a big mouthful of dirty
water almost at once upon her arm appeared a rather large rash
which Michelle started to scratch and scratch and scratch and
the more Michelle scratched the bigger the rash became and the
Bigger the rash became the more Michelle scratched (it was a
bit like a catch twenty 22 in fact) and Michelle hadn't got a
clue what to do.

It was about this time or perhaps a smidgeon before that
Michelle, began to realise she was having a very bad allergic
reaction to the water in the wishing well, it didn't help as she
noticed this she also noticed she had begun to swell and swell
at this point in the proceedings Michelle decided it was another
good opportunity to YELL so she did!!

As if things weren't bad enough, Michelle then saw her own
Reflection in the water of the wishing well. Her head had
swelled to such an extent that her head now resembled a rather
Large pumpkin on Hallowe'en night and believe you me it
wasn't a pretty sight.

When it appeared things couldn't get any worse for Michelle
they did! As Michelle had realised she had also begun to smell
this virtually spelled the death knell for poor old Michelle
because one thing she hated above all was to smell.

Continued over the page:

So Michelle, feeling unwell, smelling and looking like hell,
Decided this was another good opportunity to YELL.
Luckily all this yelling, which reverberated throughout the wishing well like a bell was heard by a passing witch who on hearing Michelle's yells looked down the wishing well and seeing her plight instantly cast a magic spell over Michelle that Made her well.
So well in fact you could never tell that Michelle had ever swelled or smelled or looked or felt like hell. In fact Michelle looked so well, when she emerged from the wishing well, she looked like the bell of the ball, and all the boys drooled and said, 'Michelle you look wonderful,' but to be honest Michelle, having fallen down the wishing well in the first place, still felt like a bit of a fool and not in the slightest bit cool.
After that Michelle went into her shell and never went near the wishing well ever again.
Oh well, we're glad you're feeling better Michelle and we all wish you well. Oh and one more thing Michelle, try not to dwell on falling down the wishing well that's a good girl.

And that is the story of the girl that fell down the wishing well.

And if you've learned anything at all from this tale I hope it's that the golden rule of sitting on the edge of a wishing well,
Is......... don't fall!
If I were you Michelle I'd sue the local council for not putting an adequate health & saftey sign on the side of the wishing well as well!

SaT NaV FoR KiDs

Get up to bed,
Get down to work,
Don't hang around,
Don't shirk
Don't get left behind,
Don't push in front
Make sure you do it right.
No wonder my head's in a spin
And I look such an awful sight.
I wish my parents would make up their minds
In which direction they want me to go
Because at the moment I don't know whether
I'm coming or going half the time.
Perhaps for Xmas they could buy me a Sat Nav
Because at the moment they're driving me
Completely out of my mind!

Ex T-ReX(TeN ReAsOnS tHe T-ReX BeCaMe ExTiNcT)

1 . A witch put a rather large hex on the T-Rex and
   Ex-spelled it.

2. The T-Rex wasn't wearing its Rolex so didn't know its
   Time was up. (Well it was a bit of an old dinosaur!!)

3. The T-Rex was ex-terminated by the Daleks.

4. The T- Rex didn't much like doing what rhymes with
   Posh & Becks!

5. The T-Rex got sucked into a deep vortex in space by a
   Giant extractor fan used in an experiment by an extra
   -Terrestrial race that went ever so slightly wrong.

6. The T-Rex became a little perplexed when it ran into a
   Door made of perplex and thought to itself *I can't possibly
   Get through this so what's the point in going on?* So it
   Didn't – go on that is!

7. The T-Rex got extremely vexed and fell backwards over a
   Cliff although why the T-Rex became so vexed palaeon
   -tologists are still like the T-Rex somewhat perplexed.
   Although personally I blame the Daleks!

Continued over the page:

8. The T-Rex got run over by a woolly mammoth driving
    A rather shiny new pink corvette (I bet you didn't see
    That one coming, no nor did the T-Rex!
    Perhaps the T-Rex should have been wearing its specs!!)

9. The T-Rex got into a fight with the missing link after the
    Two had a few too many to drink while they were watching.
    The Weakest Link the T-Rex lost and became extinct.
    Pity the T-Rex didn't think before getting into a fight with
    The missing link well with a brain the size of a pea I don't
    Think thinking was the T-Rex's forte.
    Or perhaps it had anger management issues and needed to
    See a shrink.

10. The T-Rex got erased by a time traveller from the future
    With the aid of a giant bottle of Tipp-ex although why is
    Anybody's guess but as this is a nonsense rhyme I suspect
    Nobody could really careless apart from the T-Rex that is!

And those are the ten reasons the T-Rex became an ex T-Rex
And extinct at least that's what I think….. I say with a wink!

ThE TriCk tO MaGiC iS ?

The trick to magic is keeping up the suspense
When everybody knows it's all just pretence.

The trick to magic is believe
And always leave one more trick up your sleeve.

The trick to magic is never miss a trick
i.e. never be afraid to steal another magician's trick
and pass it off as your own (that's a dirty trick!)

The trick to magic is surprise
And the hand deceiving the eyes.

The trick to magic is never admit to anyone
How you do the trick or the magic circle
Will almost certainly serve you with a writ!

The trick to magic is as a magician
Keeping the air of mystery,
As soon as you lose that as a magician you're history!

The trick to magic is there isn't one
It's all one great big con!

The trick to magic is, in conclusion..........
It's all just an illusion!

PeT ReGrEtS

There was a young man from Tibet
Who bought a Pterodactyl as a pet.
He did I'm afraid, let it out of its cage
Which was something he lived to regret!

Actually the young man from Tibet
Didn't live to regret it because the
Pterodactyl ate the young man from Tibet,
Well if you're going to buy a Pterodactyl as a pet
What do you expect?

MOdErN ArT

Modern art; a pile of bricks
An unmade bed
I think I'll give it a miss
And watch paint dry instead!

XmAs CrAcKeRs ArE a JoKe

The things you find in Xmas crackers
Really are a joke.

A plastic ring,
A rubber bat with floppy wings
A cat,
A silly paper hat.
A see-through red fish that moves when you put it
In the palm of your hand.
A rubber band (to wrap the joke and hat around)
A thimble for someone who'd have to be incredibly
Nimble or Tom Thumb.
A plastic car,
A key ring in the shape of a guitar.
The thing that makes the Xmas cracker crack!
Yes, if I had my way I'd take the whole box of Xmas
Crackers back and find the bloke who wrote the jokes
And stretch him on the rack!

27

A PLaY On WoRdS

To me a play on words
Is completely absurd.
Wouldn't the sound of stepping
On all those words
(especially the sharp ones)
Make it difficult for the actors to be heard?

I'm iN A FuNnY MoOd 2DaY

I'm in a funny mood today
I don't feel bright and sunny
I'm in a funny mood today
But in truth, I don't feel that funny!

A StReAm Of NoNsEnSe

Giant leaks, Bubble & Squeak,
Bebo & Sticky beaks.
Love shack, Tic-tacs,
Knick-knacks & Useless facts.
Hogwarts, *Red Dwarf,*
Monster trucks & Liquorice all sorts.
Quantum Mechanics, Catch 22,
Gobbledegook & Mr Magoo.
Pot bellied pigs, Long guitar licks,
The Great Rock 'n' Roll Swindle, & Flying fish.
Fu Manchu, Chopper bikes,
Pumpkin pies, & Scooby Doo.
Philatelists, Duck-billed Platypuses,
Crusty the clown & Hospital gowns.
The Big bang, Boomerangs,
The Can Can & Splodgenessabounds.
Flunkies, The Arctic monkeys,
The Simpsons & Zaphod Beeblebrox 2.
Hocus pocus, A Swarm of Locusts,
Nostradamus & Bandicoots.
Hoochie coochie, Hullabaloo,
Higgledy-Piggledy & Didgeridoos,

Continued over the page:

Dennis the Menace, *The Merchant of Venice*,
Bowler Hats & Kung Fu.
Poo-Bah, Quasar,
Zanzibar, & Dr Who.
Polygon, Wobbegong,
CD Rom & BOO!
Happy Days, Hampton Court Maze,
Purple Haze & Muse.
Hula hoops, Spondulicks,
Pookiesnackenburger & Katmandu.
Smeg heads, Egg heads,
Hot rods & i-pods too.
Aardvarks, Car parks,
Smart cars & Zoos.
Gorillaz, Zingzillas,
Album track fillers & Wallaroos.
Vuvuzelas, Bespoked tailors,
Loudhailers & Bugaboo.
Little Britain, Fingerless mittens,
Groucho Marks & Rubik cubes.
The Sonic hedgehog, Komodo dragons,
Slartibartfast, & You Tube.
Space hoppers, Glow worms,
Heroes & Einstein A Go-Go's 2.
Knickerbocker Glories, King Kong,
The Old Curiosity Shop & Full Stops!

A Spider's Much More Scared Of You Than You Are Of Him!

Don't make such a fuss and din
Because a spider's much more scared of you
Than you are of him.
So, you don't believe that's true!
Well, has a spider ever stepped on you?
Or flushed you down the loo?
Or squashed you with its shoe?
No, well then the next time you see a spider

Let's have a little less of all that Hullabaloo.
Look I'm not spinning you a yarn
Just stay calm don't be alarmed
After all a spider's not harming anyone, least of all you.
And after all that if you're still mythering on
Then I suggest when you die, you come back
Reincarnated as a spider and then tell me I'm wrong!

A WiZaRd WiTh WoRdS

I know it sounds absurd but haven't you heard
I'm a wizard with words.
And when I cast my spell over them
I can make them appear and disappear right before
Your very eyes – surprised?
Well, don't be, and it's not a trick of the light
You don't believe me?
Well be prepared to eat humble pie
And with the aid of a pen and some invisible ink and time,
This wizard with words will once again be proved right!

And if I'm not I should be expelled from the Wizipedia
Site with a spell check and thrown down a dark, dank,
Deep, dirty wishing well from a very great height!

CoUnTiNg KeNniNg RhYmE

Ten.   Bird watchers Twitching.
Nine.   Rappers Bitchin`
Eight.   Criminals Snitching.
Seven.   *Harry Potter* characters Quidditching.
Six.   Computers Glitching.
Five.   Witches Bewitching.
Four.   Grannies Stitching.
Three.   Sea planes Ditching.
Two.   Baseball players Pitching.
& One.   Flea circus owner Itching all the time
          In this counting kenning rhyme!

ThE ChiCkEn Or tHe EgG?

What came first, the chicken or the egg?
'Well why don't you ask the chicken,'
The egg said seeing red,
'Coz I'm fed up with being asked that question
And now I'm going back to bed!'

ThE PriMoRdiAL SoUp

Question: What was the first soup ever made?

Answer: The Primordial soup.

          (the one made with single celled amoebas
          And spaghetti hoops!)

If ReiNcArNaTeD WhAt WoULd YoU Be?

If reincarnated what would you be?
Would you be a hippopotamus or would you be a flea?
Or perhaps a flea's not your cup of tea
And you'd rather be a snail or a humpback whale
Or maybe an alpaca or perhaps a gnu
Or maybe an aardvark, would that suit you?

If reincarnated what would you be?
Would you be a baboon out of his tree?
Or maybe a skunk that's getting in a funk or perhaps
A gorilla in the mist would be something on your list
Or maybe a koala bear that's just a little miffed
Or perhaps a bird would be something that you'd like
Unless you simply haven't got a head for heights.

If reincarnated what would you be?
Would you be a sloth trying to show some growth
Or perhaps a duck-billed platypus trying to strike a pose
Or maybe a cow because in India they're feted
Or a great white shark that was feeling quite elated
Or maybe a komodo dragon trying to stay on the wagon
Or perhaps a pot bellied pig could be something you could dig.

If reincarnated what would you be?
The possibilities are seemingly endless I think you'd agree,
But which one would you choose given the opportunity,
Yes if reincarnated what would you be?

LeFt iN tHe ShAdE

As far as I'm concerned the sun hat
Is the best hat that's ever been made
In fact I'd go as far as to say
The sun hat leaves all the other hats in the shade!

SpiDErS WoULdN't HaRm A FLy

They say spiders are a pest
Though I don't know why
All the spiders I know
Wouldn't harm a fly!

ThE HaDrOn ColLiDeR

The Hadron Collider is full of the following things:

A dragon with great big wings,
A spider
A man eating tiger
A balsawood glider,
A crateful of cider,
A bottle of Tizer,
And a cardboard cut out of Capt. James T. Kirk,
And that is why the Hadron Collider does not work!

This rhyme was written after the Hadron Collider
Failed to work properly after its first test run
By the time this book is published it may well be
Working like a dream
Or the scientists may well have scored a massive own goal
When we all get swallowed up by a giant black hole!

The Hadron Collider was recently successfully switched on but
Will have to go through a lot more tests before it recreates the
Big Bang as it searches for the so-called God particle.
We wait with baited breath!

LiTtLe MiSs GrUmPs

Little Miss Grumps has got the hump again,
No wonder she hasn't got any friends.
She **stomps, pouts, screams and shouts**
Leaving nobody in any doubt that she's about.

Little Miss Grumps looks completely bored
When she opens the door and looks down her nose at you
As if you're nothing more than a piece of dirt upon her shoe.
Standing there in her pink and white striped tights and
Fashionable red pumps, frankly I just wish little Miss Grumps
Would take a running jump.

Little Miss Grumps has got the hump again
It's her birthday tomorrow and for her birthday
I'd like nothing more than to give her the mumps
Or anything that means she gets covered in
Itchy scratchy lumps
Then with the help of my friends we'd all give her the bumps.
Yes, then little Miss Grumps would really come crashing
Back down to earth with a bump!

Little Miss Grumps has got the hump again
Unfortunately now she's given us the hump too.
So as an extra special present we've all clubbed together
And given little Miss Grumps the flu!!

ThiNgS ThAt WilL ALwAyS Be CoOL

Cool will always be cool
Love shack by the B 52s
Che Guevara and pool
Surfing will always be cool
Sunglasses and skinny dipping too
Elvis in the 1950s banana pancakes and milkshakes
Rock with or without the roll
Skateboards and Marilyn Monroe
Kissing will always be cool
Roller coaster rides & River Phoenix too
James Dean backpacking fast cars electric guitars
And rock stars
Time travel will always be cool
James Brown J.F.K. Monty Python & *The Mighty Boosh*
The Amazon jungle Jimi Hendricks Einstein & Scooby Doo
Girls in short skirts motorbikes punk & walking on the moon
The beach faded blue jeans bedroom walls
And teen magazines
Dolphins Kirk Cobain swimming with sharks
& computer games
Parachute jumps Mexico ice gems & friends
Magic vampires Grace Kelly & tattoos too
Things that will always be cool
Well the list is endless and when all's said and done
Is pretty much down 2 U!

I've Got Spirits in My House

I've got spirits in my house
That like to move my things about.
They hide my socks, they hide my shoes
And where they put them I've not a clue.
And what am I suppose to do
When they sneak up behind me and then go

I've got spirits in my house,
They've moved right in and they won't move out.
Now some people say it's just not true,
The only spirits are inside you,
Like whisky vodka scotch and gin
When finding bottles in my bin.
Yes I've got spirits in my house,
I don't want them in, I want them out!
They're leading me a merry old dance
I just don't stand a ghost of a chance.
I cannot get a wink of sleep,
These spirits are driving me to drink
I wish these spirits would let me be
Then I'd get back to drinking tea!

NeVeR GrApPLe WiTh An ApPLe

Never grapple with an Apple
Never stare at a Pear (no don't you dare)
Never moon at a Prune (especially in June)
Never get into a drama with a Banana.
Never go to tea with a Kiwi (fruit)
Never tell a Grape it looks out of shape.
Never preach to a Peach.
Never take a dig at a Fig.
Never call a Plumb dumb.
Never get into a debate with a Date.
And never write a nonsense rhyme with the word Orange in
Because if you do you'll be completely wasting your time
Unless of course the Orange you're trying to rhyme is a
.................................Clementine!

WoRdS CaN ReAlLy HuRt

Sticks and stones will break my bones
But words will never hurt me,
Or so I've often heard it said.
Unless of course a dictionary falls off a book shelf
And lands upon your head, OUCH!

ThOnGs ArE WrOnG

There was a young man from Hong Kong
Who wore a very tight thong
He said is it right to wear it so tight
The answer is no it's all wrong!

SpAcE VeRsEs PLaNeT EaRtH

It's hard to grasp the gravity of any situation
when you're standing on a space station!

———————

Black holes are a waste of space!

———————

In recent years the price of space travel
has sky rocketed!

———————

What's an astronauts favourite salad - Rocket!

———————

Earth if you don't want to be destroyed
I would try and avoid
getting hit by a giant rogue asteroid!

———————

Here's a funny thing
Saturn's got a new ring
and as planet rings go
I must admit it's pretty impressive bling!

———————

ThE HaUnTeD HoUsE

The Haunted House is as quiet as a mouse
Until it hears Creeks and Squeaks, then it Shrieks!
And hides under the sheets until finally it Peeks
Before eventually getting back off to sleep.

The Haunted House is as quiet as a mouse,
Until it gets spooked, then it gets Jumpy.
It's heart Thumps, it gets goose Bumps
And in fear puts its fingers in its ears
And hopes the scary noises all just disappear.

The Haunted House is as quiet as a mouse,
Until it hears an Owl Hoot, then it can be found
Quaking in its boots and if it wasn't rooted to the spot,
It would probably just Scoot!

The Haunted House is as quiet as a mouse,
Until it wakes in the middle of the night,
With a fright and turns on all its lights
To avoid getting too uptight then starts to write
Its own life story which by the way is pretty gory
With the aid of a Ghost writer of course,
As well it might.

Continued over the page:

The Haunted House is as quiet as a mouse,
Well actually it's not that's just rot.
It's full of Ghouls and Ghosts burning the toast,
Spirits and Apparitions coming through the partitions,
Moans Groans and mobile phones,
Shrieks and Shouts, teenagers running about.
Bumps in the night, flashing lights,
Poltergeists that aren't very nice.
Blood curdling SCREAMS, vanishing cream,
Nightmares, creaking stairs, Geeks caught unaware
Floating books I can't bear to look!
Let's face it, the Haunted House is anything but as quiet
As a mouse, it's more like a noisy public house,
Full of Spirits during Hallowe'en at happy hour
If you know what I mean!

(You don't? well then may I suggest you go and watch
   Scream 3 in HD on your 3D TV!!)
   I just hope your house is not haunted…... sleep tight!!)

I HaTe AlL PuNcTuAtiOn FULL STOP!

I hate commas and FULL STOPS
They just slow me down when I'm on a roll
And stop my ebb and flow
And I wish they'd all just go away and leave me alone
So I can carry on writing 'till the cows come home!

WhAt'S A PrObOsCiS?

A Proboscis sounds quite funny
A Proboscis sounds quite weird
But what a Proboscis is
Well I've really got no idea!

A DuCk-BilLeD PLaTyPuS CuSsiNg

Imagine if a duck-billed platypus had a mind to cuss,
Think of all the fuss it would cause.
And people would be in a rush to stare and say
'Look over there. Where? Over there there's a
Duck-billed platypus cussing I swear!
Have you ever seen such a thing in your life before?
It should be against the law.'
But after a while it would become a bit of a bore
And some people would just smile and say,
'A Duck-billed platypus cussing oh that's alright,
He's probably got tourette's the poor little mite.
Anyway I've heard worse

I've heard a racoon rant,
An anteater bleat,
I've heard a grizzly bear swear
I've heard a centipede use expletives like you wouldn't believe
And that's some feet, sorry feat I'd think you'd agree.
I've heard a rat say "shut your trap"
I've seen and heard a Bandicoot dish out some awful abuse
And turn the air blue.

Continued over page:

I've heard a chuckawalla curse and worse
I've seen a tiger of the sabre tooth variety in truth
Be quite uncouth,
And heard a great white shark make some quite
Biting remarks.
So a duck-billed platypus cussing is, to me,
Nothing new and a lot of fuss about nothing
After all we all have to let off steam somehow, don't we?'

The author would like to make it perfectly clear that
He doesn't condone cussing in any shape or form.
Unless you've just dropped *The Complete Works of
Shakespeare* on your foot and in doing so have broken
Your metatarsal, thus missing the schools F.A. Cup final.
In which case by all means cuss away to your heart's content!
(But probably best to do it under your breath!!)

OnE SaNdWiCh ShoRt Of A PiCniC

A caterpillar can make a very good sandwich filler,
If you've got nothing else to put inside your bread,
But I wouldn't advise using a moth,
It will only make you cough and splutter unless,
You're using plenty of butter, or it's already dead!
A snail is definitely an acquired taste but is no substitute
For a good sandwich paste, I think it's fair to say.
And unless of course you prefer a good juicy pest
(Like a bird-eating spider) then perhaps it's best
To stick to a caterpillar as a sandwich filler
And simply forget the rest!

BLiNdEd By SciEnCe

Now I've left school
I can say with some defiance,
My chemistry teacher use to
Blind me with science!

LiCk Me iNtO ShApE

I'm a lolly
That needs to lose some weight
So please feel free
To lick me into shape!

SaLaAm'S LoSt tHe PLoT

The Devil really lost the plot
The day someone sold old Salaam's lot.
Whoever did the dirty deed
Would die at the hands of the Devil's seed.
Whoever did the hard sell,
The Devil swore they'd rot in hell.
'The Devil's plot was not for sale,'
The Devil said as he stroked his tail
'Instead why not buy the Holy Grail?
I hear it's going cheap at a car boot sale!'

ChiNeSe WhiSpErS

Pass it around, yesterday I heard a
Chinese whisper in the school playground

Pass it around, yesterday someone found a
Chinese man with big whiskers in the school playground.

Pass it round, yesterday Miss Twister the headmaster's
Sister, was found kissing a Chinese man with big whiskers
In the school playground.

Pass it round, yesterday someone found a Chinese man
Whispering to the headmaster about having a big blister
On his foot, while his sister was shaving her whiskers
In the school playground.

Pass it round, yes I know someone heard a Chinese whisper
In the school playground and everybody passed it around,
Hold on a minute don't make a sound I think I hear another
Chinese whisper in the school playground let's hope this one
Is a little more profound!

I'm   BoReD!

I'm alone in the house and I'm bored,
Along with the cat that can't be bothered to chase the mouse.
The wood on the floor that's board too
Along with the loo that's a little flushed and hasn't really got
much else to do.
The iron's bored along with the phone cord.
The lawn's so bored it can't be bothered to grow,
Along with the snow that can't be bothered to melt.
And I can't be bothered to go out to play in the snow
Because it's too cold.
The TV's bored of being switched off and on.
The birds are so bored they can't be bothered to make a sound.
The rain's so bored it's falling up instead of down.
I'm so bored I've even got time to burn the toast
And I'll tell you who else is bored in this house, the ghost!
He, like the phone, is so bored he can't even be bothered
To moan and groan.
The dog's so bored it can't even be bothered to chew on
Its bone.
Even the garden gnomes are bored and can't be bothered
To roam.
And it must be catching to because the banks are so bored
They can't be bothered to give anybody a bank loan!
And I never thought I'd hear myself say this, but I'm now
So bored I can't wait for my little sister to come home!

SeE YoU LaTeR AlLiGaToR

Which would you prefer as a pet
An alligator or a crocodile?
Answer – a crocodile by a mile
With its great big beaming smile
And warm embrace.
Yes, a crocodile has exceptionally good taste.
And although an alligator would be happy
To meet you
Sooner or later it's bound to eat you!
So it's see you later alligator
And I'll see you in a while crocodile!

A StOrM iN A TeACuP

Wouldn't it make it difficult to sup
If there was a storm in a teacup?

A PoEm FoR An InSoMniAc

Not counting sheep to go to sleep
Counting stars to go to bed instead!

NoT A CLuE

I haven't got a clue how to do a crossword have you?

YoU're OnLy MaKiNg A
SpEcTaCLe Of YOuRsELf

Where are my glasses?
Where can they be?
Without them I just cannot see.
I've hunted high and low
I've looked under my pillow behind my cello
I'm tempted to ask if I can borrow the glasses
Of England manager Fabio Cappello
I shout holla and bellow and normally I'm so mellow
And such a hail and hearty fellow.
But now I've started to wallow
So with my spirits low off to bed I go
Only to find my glasses it has to be said
Still sitting there perched on the top of my head!

Mind you after the World Cup I'm not sure I'd want to
borrow the glasses of Fabio Cappello!
And they say you can see the Great Wall of China from
Outerspace, but apparently not the fact Frank Lampard's
shot was five feet over the line!!
Perhaps a certain referee and linesman should have gone
to Optical Viewing Device Savers!!

A WiNtEr HaiKu

The tree stood quietly
While winter slowly crept in
Leaving the tree bare

A HaiKu

Haiku's are poems
Of seventeen syllables
Written in three lines

Haiku footnote: The first line has five
The second line has seven
The last line has five

My TeAcHeR's GoT A MeSsY DeSk

My teacher's got a messy desk of which of course
She does protest.
She says she hasn't got the time to clear it up
Is such a bind.
She didn't mean to leave the cups, she really ment
To wash them up.
And all those papers and files and stuff and all the
Other silly guff.
Of course I sympathised with her plight but,
'Miss,' I said, 'it's just not right, to leave the cups
There in plain site.
After all a messy desk equals a messy mind perhaps
Miss, it would help to bare that in mind,
And the next time take your own advice because you tell
Us kids not to make a mess but it seems you've failed
Your own strict test.
And I really don't want to be a pest
But Miss you've got a messy desk,
And I really don't want to be to harsh,
But Miss you're bottom of the class.
And Miss if I had to mark your desk
Then Miss I'd simply give you…. an F!'

On the subject of having a messy desk
I just hope I've got Miss's attention
And now she's learned her lesson otherwise
Soon Miss will find herself in detention!!

BeWaRE Of CrOcODiLeS

A crocodile can smile with its big wide grin
And if you get too close it will happily fit you in.
So you've got to be careful when crocodiles are around
Because they're faster than they look
And they hardly make a sound.
Apart from the snapping of their great big jaws
As they swallow you down
And the grinding of their teeth on your disappearing feet.
And here's a little fact that happens to be true
Crocodiles eat people more than sharks ever do!
So if you're in the outback always watch your back
Or on the crocodiles menu you'll end up as a snack!

MaKiNg A POiNt

!

'I was only trying to make a point
but I think I may have gone a little too far,'
exclaimed the exclamation mark!

ThErE's A SpiDeR iN tHe BaTh!

'There's a spider in the bath!'
I hear my sister shout.
'Don't just stand there looking at it
Just get the dam thing out.'

'There's a spider in the bath,
I just can't bear to look.

Just turn its lights out now,' she shouts,
'Yes bash it with a book.'

'There's a spider in the bath,
It's really moving fast.
Just get it out,' my sister cries,
As I begin to laugh.

There's a spider in the bath,
Well actually there's not.
I turned the taps both on full blast
And that was the spider's lot!

Personally I think my sister should just man up!
after all everybody knows a spiders much more
scared of you than you are of him!!

BLiNg'S ThEiR ThiNg

Magpies have a thing,
A thing for collecting bling,
Every blinging shiny thing,
Including wedding rings
Hidden in their nests along with all the rest,
To them its like a treasure chest,
The thieving little pests.
Silver bling,
Gold bling,
Bling both large and small,
Expensive bling,
Minging bling,
Diamond bling and all.
Bling that's tacky bling that's cool,
Bling that's old bling that's new,
Even bling that's tat,
All manner of bling in fact.
Yes, magpies have a thing,
A thing for collecting bling
And if a magpie stole my bling
I'd really be upset
And if I got my hands on it I'd wring its blinging neck!

PoEtRy iN MoTiOn

Poetry in motion as a notion
To me doesn't make much sense.
Unless of course you're reading your poetry
On a plane, bus or train then of course it does!

A RiGhT NuMpTy

Humpty Dumpty
Sat on a wall

Humpty Dumpty
Had a great fall

Humpty Dumpty,
A right numpty,
One brick short of a wall!

A WoMbAt iS WhErE iT's At

A Wombat is not a rat.
It's not a cat.
It's neither a womble
Or a bat or for that matter in fact
Any variety of bat be it fruit or ding.
It's a wombat and a wombat is where it's at
(Even if it is a little off the beaten track).
And I don't mean to get ratty or scatty or even catty
But confusing it with other animals or mammals or manimals
Is driving me batty and that's a fact!
(Yes a Wombat is where it's at
At last finally I think we're on the right track.)

To Me MaThS SiMpLy DoEsN't AdD Up

To me maths simply doesn't add up
It's just one number after another.
And no matter how hard I try
I just can't figure it out.
And I'm sorry but I don't give a hoot
About the square root
Or a monkey's about the hippopotamuse
Or whatever the damn thing's called alright.
Yes to me maths simply doesn't add up.
Mind you if I won the lottery
I think it just might!

SaNtA BaNtA

I hear Santa works one day a year,
The rest of the year he disappears,
Along with the rest of his reindeers
And sits in all his red and white gear,
Watching dvds and eating pizza
And drinking cold beer,
Until the same time next year.
No wonder his retirement is getting near
And if you look closely at his rear
Then I think you can see why that's pretty clear!

(I could be wrong but perhaps Santa's got a clause in his
  contract whereby he has to wear red all year long!)

My FriEnDs ArE SuCh LiTtLe GeMs

My friends are such little gems,
Like ruby, emerald and sapphire,
All of which I admire and will never tire,
But my best friend is a real diamond
On whom I can always depend,
Because as they say,
Diamonds are a girl's best friend.

DoN'T StiFLe A GiGgLe

Don't stifle a giggle,
Loosen it a little
And let it wriggle on out
To play happily on a roundabout.

Don't stifle a laugh
And hide it behind a mask
Or let it get eaten by a great white shark
Yes that would simply be daft.

Don't stifle a smile even for a little while.
Don't keep it off your dial
Or let it float away down the River Nile,
Or file it away for another day.
Let it come out to play.

Don't stifle a chuckle
And keep it locked up deep inside you
With the aid of your belt buckle,
Or let it be taken away from you
On a roller coaster ride now where's your pride?

Don't stifle a chortle
And let it fall down some time portal
After all you're not immortal.

Continued over the page:

Don't stifle a smirk,
You berk,
Beam just like Capt. James T. Kirk.

Don't stifle a snigger
And keep it under your hat
Or leave it with your spare keys under the mat,
Surely you're bigger than that,
Why not grin like a Cheshire cat.

Don't stifle a titter.
Or let it be taken off by some strange critter.
Or throw it away like litter.
Do you want to end up twisted and bitter.
Yes don't fritter it away
Or sell it on ebay
Why not put it on Twitter?

Don't stifle a grin
Or throw it in the waste paper bin
No that would be a sin.

Don't stifle a roar or let it fall on the floor
Or sneak out the backdoor
Or bury it deep in the earth's core
No don't be such an infernal bore.

So if you want to win just grin, roar, snigger,
Smirk, laugh, titter, chuckle, smile, chortle, giggle
For if you don't it'll niggle you forevermore!

A SnAkE's A ReAL ChArMeR

A Snake exudes a lot of charm
And will rarely ever do you harm.
So feel free to hold its head in the palm of your hand
And don't be disarmed if it wraps itself around your arm
Just stay calm.
Yes, don't become a nervous wreck
Well at least not until it becomes a little bolder
And then slides up onto your shoulder.
Then as you start to sweat
I'd freely have to admit a snake's nothing………….
But a pain in the neck!

ThiNgS tHaT ScArE tHe PaNtS OfF Of YoU!

A Nightmare,
A Vampire's stare.
A Grizzly Bear.
A burst balloon
A Spider you've found in your bedroom,
A Werewolf howling at the Moon.
A large Rat,
A flapping blood sucking Bat , A hissing Cat,
A Shark ready to attack.
Wild Geese,
Your Grandad's false teeth.
In a jet plane an ejector seat.
A charging Bull,
Having your tooth pulled,
The teacher that's a Dragon at your school.
A Sky dive,
An angry Bee hive,
A Roller coaster ride,
Frankenstein's bride,
A Ghost train ride when you're five.
The Hadron Collider,
A Sabre tooth Tiger.
Heights,
Your imagination when you turn out your bedroom light.
Clowns, large baying hounds,
Yes, these are some of the things that scare the pants off of you
     …………….and me too!!

An ElAbOrAtE JoKe

Question: What did an 18th century furniture maker
Eat for breakfast?

Answer: Rococo Pops!

Footnote: Rococo 18th century elaborate decoration
Or furniture.

AdViCe On WhAt tO Do iF YoU FiNd A SLeEpiNg TiGeR OuT iN ThE SuN

Here's some advice on what to do if you find a Sleeping tiger out in the sun.

A. Thank your lucky stars it's asleep for one

& B. (Before it wakes up, and this isn't rocket science) …

.... RUN!!!

MOnEy TaLkS

They say money talks.
Well, I don't agree,
Because if it does it never talks to me.
When money sees me it walks across to the
Other side of the street.
(The one with the cash machine
On the corner presumably!).
Perhaps it would pay me to offer money
A small fee, then maybe,
Money would talk to me!
(Yes I agree that would be pretty drastic,
Still there's always plastic!).

I'Ve LoSt My VOiCe

I've lost my voice I can't find it anywhere.
Did I leave it in the cupboard under the stairs
Or did it fall down the side of the armchair.
Either way I'm tearing out my hair.
Did I leave it in the laundry basket along with my
Dirty underwear or did my partner Clare take it
When we broke up along with my cuddly old teddy bear?
Either way it's not fair and I'm thinking of giving my
Family and friends a questionnaire to help me find my voice.
But just as I was beginning to fear for my own welfare,
A little voice inside my head, said *did you look under the bed*?
So I went upstairs and there was my voice giving me a
withering glare weakly saying to me *I thought you no
Longer cared.*
My voice must have fallen out when I was having
That violent nightmare last night, what a relief!
Now if only I could find my glasses and my false teeth!

iN ShOrT, BoXeRs ArE PaNtS

Pants are pants
But not as pants as boxer shorts
They're really pants
But not as pants as briefs
And don't even get me started on thongs
Thongs are just wrong
So in brief or in short
which ever you prefer
And I don't mean to get my knickers in a twist or rant
But boxers are pants!

WeLcOmE To tHe PoEtRy ShOp

Welcome to the poetry shop,
Here you can shop until you drop.
Have a look round feel free to stop.
(Here there's no need to watch the clock).
Yes, welcome to the poetry shop.

We have poems of all sizes and shapes.
We have poems to suit all tastes.
Sad ones, happy ones short and long,
Yes, we have poems for everyone.

Feel free to browse just take your time.
We have in stock a, million rhymes.
We've limericks, odes, couplets galore,
Stanzas, verses all here in store.
And if you need some help just shout
And we'll only be too happy to help you out.

Welcome to the poetry shop.
So glad you took the time to stop.
We hope you had a lovely day
And will enjoy the poems you're taking away.

FaSt FoOdS

Runny fried eggs,

Fried chicken legs,

Hamburgers,

Fries,

Runner beans,

Any quick bite,

Yes these are the fast foods that I like!

WhAt CaN U BuY On ebAy 2DaY

What can you buy on ebay today?
A hat, a toast rack, a worn-out mat.
A splat the rat (not necessarily intact).
A cricket bat. A video of Postman Pat.
You could probably even sell your own cat,
No perhaps you'd better scratch that!
A black and white cow that goes *moo*.
E. T. (the dvd, well you didn't think it was the real
E.T. did you?)
An old leather jacket. A stringless tennis racket.
A cd by Keen. A lean mean grilling machine (that's
Never been cleaned!).
A beer mat signed by the queen!
An extinct dinosaur that's recently been thawed.
A door into a parallel universe (that one you can't afford!)
Madonna's purse (with authentic paperwork)
A life size cardboard cut out of Capt. James T. Kirk.
A toothache (now that's got to be fake and who'd buy it
Anyway?...............you'd be surprised!!)
A broken garden rake.
A half eaten jar of marmalade.
The Titanic made of papier-maché.
A book on feng shui. An ice cream Sunday.
A locke of Elvis's hair. Fresh air!
An old cuddly teddy bear.
The Blue Planet on blu-ray.
What can you buy on ebay today, more like what can't you
Buy on ebay today virtually nothing, I'd have to say,
Now how do I pay?

ThAt'S A LOt Of CAtS (BuT HoW mAnY?)

If six cats from Catford called Kit,
All had six kittens called Cat,
Who then had six kittens called Kit,
Who then had six kittens called Cat,
Which is a lot of kittens and a lot of cats.
But how many kittens and how many cats in fact
Did the six cats from Catford and their offspring
Actually have?

I do hope that's purr-fectly clear!

Answer: A lot of Cats and a lot of kittens and that a fact!!
How many?….. How would I know? I'm a poet not
A mathematician have you ever heard of a calculator?
If you ever find the answer out don't tell me because
I'll be having a cat nap, then watching *Glee*,
Then playing on my nephew's Wii before trying to
Write a rhyme about a…………spelling bee!!

ThE SpElLiNg BEE

I am the Spelling Bee so come over here and spell for me.
Right, I want you to spell the word Honey
H-o-n-e-y. that's correct, you're right on the money.
Now can you spell the word Bee for me.
B-E no not that be are you completely out of your tree?
Everybody knows there are two 'e's in Bee
Do you want me to sting you on the knee?
And that won't be metaphorically!!
I'm sorry but that's it you're done
So you may as well go outside and play in the sun.
Or play indoors on your Wii.
Or watch *Glee*.
Yes, you're out of the Spelling Bee so please just buzz off
Or you won't get any honey tonight for your tea,
Right next please.
And your word is Hive yes that's right hive
The place that I reside. H-i-v-e. that's right you've survived,
Sorry now I've got to fly because the beekeeper has arrived.
Oh and next time you come to the Spelling Bee do you think
You could possibly wear a tie?

CaRs ArE SmArT?

Cars are big,
Cars are small,
Cars are naff,
Cars are cool,
Cars are slow,
Cars are fast,
Cars are dirty,
Cars are smart.

Yes they're smart alright
So smart they regularly get stuck behind tractors
And dirty smelly horse and carts!
Yes after that smart cars are not so smart
No not smart enough by half!

ThAt'S BaNaNaS

I don't like eating bananas
While they're still wearing their clothes
But I don't want to peel them off
In case they feel over-exposed!

ThAt'S BaNaNaS 2

I like eating bananas
Including eating their skins
Or perhaps it's just that I'm lazy
That I eat the whole blimin' thing!

ThE TaLe Of ThE FaiRy

This is the tale of the fairy who lived in a fairy tale.
In this fairy tale unfortunately there's no good
Pretending, there is no fairy tale ending,
For the fairy in this fairy tale ended up in jail.
And it's no fairy tale spending time in a modern over
crowded jail,
The fairy having failed to make bail for not paying
Her council tax, and then spent the next eighteen
Months sewing tags onto mail bags with a bunch
Of hardened old lags by the names of Cinderella,
Little Red Riding hoodie, three pigs who shall remain
Nameless and the big bad wolf,
Who to be fair, wasn't all that bad,
He was just a bit of a lad that got mixed up with The
Wrong Crowd, a few chav's with the liking for white
cider and selling knock off dvds.
Hardly an offence where they were ever going to
Throw away the keys.
Eighteen months later the fairy left jail,
Having paid her debt to society.

Continued over the page:

Unfortunately the day she was released from jail
There was a force ten gale and she was blown a very,
very long way away, the Pacific Ocean to be
More precise and was swallowed by a Humpback
Whale who was trying to catch his own tail.
Like I said unfortunately this fairy's fairy tale has
No fairy tale ending apart from this ending..........
The End!!

My DaD SnOrEs LoUdEr ThAn A DiNoSaUr

My dad snores louder than a dinosaur,
Louder than a wild boar charging across the floor boards
Louder than a dragons roar.
When my dad snores it's like a third world war
Or a grizzly bear with a thorn in its paw.
Yes when dad snores it's impossible to ignore that's for sure.
The whole house shakes.
It's like an earthquake. Make no mistake,
There's enough wind coming from my dad's mouth to blow
Out the candles on an octogenarian's birthday cake.
Now everybody's awake.
The noise is like a sonic boom.
Me and my sister have taken to sleeping in the bathroom,
But frankly we'd have more chance
Of sleeping in a vampire's tomb.
Yes, when dad snores it's all doom and gloom.
My brother has taken to sleeping in the garden shed
Instead of sleeping in his own bed.
The lodger is sleeping in a tent.
Well, at least for him it saves on the rent.
Still my dad's tossing and turning surely as he sleeps
His ears must be burning.
My mum's in tears, we all put cotton wool in our ears
(even my brother who's sleeping in the garden shed)
And hope the dreadful noise disappears.

Continued over the page:

And I don't mean to be unkind, but my dad's snoring is
Worse than a children's pantomime!
Surely his snoring is against the law.
Even a loud rock band couldn't compete.
We're all so tired we're almost out on our feet.
When he snores it sounds worse than the waste disposal
Unit in the kitchen sink and it's driving us all to drink.
And I think the only way we're going to get a decent nights
Sleep I say with a wink, is if my dad,
Like the dinosaur, becomes extinct!!

BoXiNg CLeVeR

My name's Trevor
And so I don't get hurt ever,
I'm boxing with my shadow.
Now that's what I call boxing clever!
Yes, very clever Trevor, but did you
Ever think in your imaginary bout your shadow
Might come out of the shadows
And knock you out?
Then it would hurt without a shadow of a doubt!

ExCuSe tHe PuN 2

I'm sure I'm not the only one
Who thought Shakespeare
Was well versed in poetry
If thou will excuse the pun!

I' m LoSt FoR WoRdS

A HiPpOpOtAmUs ThAt'S PrEpOsTeROuS

'It's quite preposterous,' said the rhinoceros,
'And it's becoming rather monotonous,
That anybody should mistake me for a hippopotamus,
For a hippopotamus is extremely obstropalous and has a
Very big bottamus and I've not,' said the rhinoceros sounding
Rather cross and at a loss as to why he should be mistaken
for a Obstropalous hippopotamus.
'I'm a great big pussy cat. Well obviously I'm not, but
I'm certainly not a hippopotamus,' said the rhinoceros getting
Rather hot under the collar and a little obstropalous.
Then one hippopotamus turned to another hippopotamus
and Said, 'Have you heard what the rhinoceros is saying
about us?'
'Yes,' said the other hippopotamus trying hard not to
create a fuss that's slanderous and completely absurd so he gave the
Rhinoceros the bird.
The rhinoceros didn't like getting the bird so gave the bird
Back to the hippopotamus who flew off in a huff. (the bird
Not the hippopotamus). The hippopotamus flying off in a huff
Now that really would have been absurd.
The rhinoceros now even more cross than it was before shouted
To the herd of hippopotamuses,
'You're a lot of obnoxious ignoramuses and have you looked in
The bathroom mirror recently?
No, I thought not.' When the herd of hippopotamuses
heard that remark they shouted back in unison, 'Talk about the pot
Calling the kettle black, you're not exactly an oil painting
Yourself mate,'

And for good measure threw in, 'Have you swallowed the
Thesaurus because if you're not careful one of these days
You're going to trip over your own tongue, after all this is the
Wild not Oxford University, you great big oaf.'
The herd of hippopotamus then drew another breath and
made yet an even more set of cutting remarks,
Which however thick-skinned the rhinoceros was, were bound
To hurt. 'Do you know how absurd you look and we'd all much
Rather be a hippopotamus than a ridiculous humourless
Posturing preposterous cantankerous rhinoceros like you,
Who seemingly hasn't got a clue and only seems happy when
He's creating a HULLABALOO!'
Then a single hippopotami who was a bit of a wit said to the
Rhinoceros, 'You're a hippo-crit.' which was like one big
Metaphorical poke in the eye for the rhinoceros who then
Started to cry.
'Never in my born days have I been spoken to in such a
fashion.'
He said, as he stormed off into the wild like a scalded
child.
At this precise moment the bird that had been given to the
Rhinoceros by the hippopotamus that in turn he'd given back
To the hippopotamus in a fit of pique, flew over his head.
'You look wild,' said the bird with his tongue firmly placed in
His beak. 'Wild?' said the rhinoceros, 'Wild, I'm livid.'
'Well that will teach you to be such a big head,' said the bird.
'You should be flattered that anybody should mistake you for
A hippopotamus. For a hippopotamus is a charming fellow and
Wouldn't say boo to a goose.'

'It's only because you've driven the hippopotamus to this rather
Uncharacteristic out burst, normally its mild and meek and
Turns the other cheek which I think you'll find in the wild
Is quite unique.'
'Did I ask you to speak?' said the rhinoceros to the bird in
Another fit of pique, as it continued to charge off into the wild
To play its own personal game of hide and seek and lick its
Wounds for the next three weeks.
The bird was only to happy to have put one final flea into the
Rhinoceroses ear so to speak.
The bird then turned tail feathers and flew back in the direction
Of the herd of hippopotamuses who were happily swimming in
The river and wallowing in the mud and as it did the bird
Thought to itself, *that's absurd that's preposterous that a
Rhinoceros should be mistaken for a hippopotamus they don't
Look in the least bit alike*................. now I'm in little
doubt
How the term bird brain came about!

Unfortunately for the author the bird saw this Tweet on Twitter
and spread the word via his Myspace page, and ever since then
he has been unable to walk in parks or walk along
seafronts without being dive bombed by a various
assortment of creatures of the feathered variety. And now
even hearing a few bars of the Birdy Song makes him fly
off the handle and dive for cover. Also the author has been
forced to give up his love for twitching (Bird watching)
and now has a twitch that is a permanent reminder to him
that birds have feelings and are human too!!
When I wrote this I did have my tongue firmly placed in
my beak, sorry I mean cheek!!

ThE ALiEnS ArE CoMiNg!

The aliens are coming,
Don't run don't panic,
They're only coming from another planet.
They're only coming from the Milky Way
And that's not very far away.

The aliens are coming,
I know it's quite frightening
And they'll soon be here as fast as lightning.
They'll soon be here in just a flash
That's, of course if at first they don't crash.

The aliens are coming,
What took them so long?
Was it their Sat Nav that went horrible wrong,
Or have they been here many times before
And are now finding it all a bit of a bore?

The aliens are coming, let's turn up the heating
And that should stop the bleeders bleating
And saying it's just to blimin' cold
And 'We're aiming are ray guns at the North Pole.'

The aliens are coming there is no doubt,
And if you like you can shout and shout,
And put your fingers in your ears
And hope they simply disappear.

Continued over the page:

The aliens are coming, please don't vomit
They're coming from behind that great big comet.
They're coming and they won't be long
To blow us all to kingdom come.

The aliens are coming
Not according to the Whitehouse
It's all been a hoax, like the *War of the Worlds*
Read by the actor Orson Welles
And the sightings are quite easily explained
They're weather balloons and flocks of geese
And other phenomena that nobody believes.

The aliens are coming, don't be silly we're alone,
We're the centre of the Universe our planet Earth, home.
And the Earth is flat and we've never been to the Moon
Yes I think you'll agree it's all doom and gloom.

The aliens are coming, just look on the website,
Oh, and please if you can try not to get uptight
And there's still time to put up a blog
And text all your friends or just pray to God.
The aliens are coming and are meeting the pope
And that I'm afraid might be our last hope.
Yes the aliens are coming, no actually they're not,
They've forgotten their ray guns and their packed lunch so
I've got a hunch they'll be back again same time next month!

ThiS iS NOt A FaIrY TaLe
(ToO MuCh DeTaiL)

Without fail a boa constrictor will have your heart rate
Going right off the Richter scale.
First you'll start to wail as around your neck it wraps its tail.
Then you'll go extremely pale. You'll start coughin'
You won't be able to exhale as your heart fails.
Your face will go red your eyes will pop out of your head
And on your final breath you'll look and feel like death,
And that will be the final nail in your coffin,
Leaving your widow standing over your grave
Wearing a black vail.
Too much detail well I'm sorry but this isn't a fairy tale
(Didn't you read the title!)

It'S nOt RoCkEt SciENcE Is It?

How come everybody panics
When they hear they've got a test
On quantum mechanics...............
After all it's not rocket science is it?

Does an astronaut go to a quantum mechanic
To get his rocket repaired?
Of course he does, it's not rocket science is it?

Footnote: Look I've got to be honest, I know about rhyming
Patterns but what I know about quantum mechanics
And rocket science you could probably fit on the
Top of an atom!!

ThErE'S An ArMaDiLlOw On My PilLOw

I've got an armadillo on my pillow
It feels like a brillo pad in fact,
But I'd much rather have a cat or a bat or an anteater
Or a gorilla on my pillow or even a rat
Than an armadillo and that's a fact.
Now I know it's a little unusual
To have an armadillo on my pillow
I think that's plain to see
But should I wake it up or just let it be?
I could do with some good advice
Or at the very least some tea and sympathy.
Perhaps I should sleep on the floor
As its started to snore
And let the armadillo sleep on the bed instead of me!

It DoEsN't HuRt tO SMiLe

It really doesn't hurt to smile
Unless you're being eaten by a crocodile!

OdE tO ReCyCLiNg

Where does all the recycling go?
I wouldn't know where to begin
But if I had to take a wild stab in the dark
I'd probably have to say straight in the bin!

ChRiStMaS

Too much food,
Too much drink,
Xmas lights on the blink,
High jinks,
Dodgy cufflinks.
Of sleep can't get a wink.
Great presents tickled pink,
Bad presents create a stink.
Relatives pushed to the brink.
Playing silly games of tiddly winks,
Desperately need forty winks!
Being forced to watch the Xmas edition of *The Weakest Link*.
Wine glasses clink,
After dinner men off to the pub slink,
To avoid washing up in the kitchen sink.
Glad Xmas is over for another year
I definitely think!

ThE WiCkEd WiTcH iS A WiZaRd
On ThE FOoTbAlL PiTcH

The Wicked Witch is a wizard on the football pitch
To see her dribbling down the wing is such a wonderful thing
And when she's playing you'll see the goals simply flying in.
And you should hear her cackle when she goes in for a tackle.
And she's not afraid to mix it by putting her foot in
Where it hurts or kick the odd attacker in the shins
Yes with the witch on your side how can you fail to win.
Mind you, your team would have to be pretty rich
To afford a player as good as the Wicked Witch.
Yes, just to hear the crowd yell
When she's having a magic spell
She can't do any wrong (apart from the fact that she pongs!)
As the spectators sing her song,
Wicked Witch, Wicked Witch
Wizard on the football pitch.
She beats one she's on a run,
She beats two, she's almost through,
She beats three she's worth that huge fee,
She beats four she scores the crowd roars.
Yes, the witch is a wizard on the football pitch that's for sure.
And as far as I'm concerned the witch is a snitch at any price
Even if at times she's not very nice.
There is of course just one small hitch
Would the F.A. allow the witch to play on the football pitch?
If I know the F.A. I'd probably have to say 'NO WAY!!'

BoTtoM Of tHe CLaSs

One of my mates shouted out to me
'You're losing your marbles,'
Just as we were walking into class,
But I ignored him, because I thought he was just being daft.
Until I got into class and found a great big hole in my pocket.
My mate was right. I was losing my marbles
No wonder I'm bottom of the class!

GiVe SaNtA tHe SaCk

If Santa doesn't bring me
What I want this year for Xmas
I'll send it all back
And give Santa the sack!

ThErE'S SoMeThiNg LiViNg iN My FriDgE

There's something living in my fridge
I think it started out as a bowl of porridge,
Or something equally horrid like a bacon and egg flan,
Or half eaten pizza, or something else I never actually
Planned to eat which would have repeated on me
For the rest of the week.
Yes, whatever it is it's now lurking at the back of my fridge
Just waiting to pounce, every time I open the fridge door.
It feels like I'm at war with some alien spore,
Leaving me wishing I was a matador or the Norwegian
God Thor to battle its long bony claw and all for a few
Stale cheese straws, and some coleslaw.
The other day I forgot it was there and it caught me on the hop,
And I had to fight it off with the kitchen mop, I barely
Survived it had grown to such an enormous size,
And you should have seen all the blood and gore on the kitchen
Floor when I tried to kill it with a chainsaw.
I think it might have metamorphosed from some left over pork
As I tried to stab it with a pitch fork.
But one day there was a respite in our fight and the thing that
Was living in my fridge that used to be a piece of pork
Started to talk. Yes it seemed that are frosty relationship was
Beginning to thaw as it poked its head round the fridge door.
It said 'Please don't harm me anymore I'm fed up with this war
I'm only trying to survive that's why, in your fridge, I hide.'
So I sang it a lullaby and it went off to sleep and now from the
Thing living in my fridge I hardly hear a peep and now we're
good friends, and I can get up in the middle of the night
without getting into a fight and eat what I like,
Now where's that angel delight?

It WaS AlL ThE RaGe iN ThE StOnE AgE

It was all the rage in the Stone Age to keep a baby
Pterodactyl in a cage or at least until the baby pterodactyl
Came of age.
Unfortunately Stone Age man could never quite gauge
At what age to take the baby pterodactyl out of its cage.
And when the baby pterodactyl came of age and was able
To engage its brain it became so enraged that it was still
Being kept in a cage it instantly flew into a rage,
And broke out of the cage, and ate the Stone Age man who
Put it in the cage.
A wise old sage was one day heard to say it was a big mistake
To put the baby pterodactyl in the cage in the first place
But by then it was far too late!
You'd have thought after a while Stone Age man would have
Learned from his mistakes.
Mind you on the whole Stone Age man was a bit of a
NEANDERTHAL!!

Authors note: I'm well aware that the dinosaur died out long
             Before man turned up on the scene but this is a
             Nonsense rhyme. So if you're a palaeontologist
             Out there tearing out their hair, chill-ax man go
             Read an article about Posh & Becks or listen to
             T. Rex because frankly I don't care!

BiG UpS

You're outta sight.
You're a pure delight.
You're cool,
You're sound,
You're the best around.
You're the best
You're better than all the rest.
When I'm around you I feel blessed.
You rock, you're the tops
You're Top of the Pops.
You're a star.
You'll go far.
You're the best cookie in the cookie jar.
You're a top banana,
A real charmer.
An absolute diamond of the 24 carat variety.
A jewel of high society.
You're the bee's knees,
A real crowd pleaser.
You're bionic.
You're supersonic.
You knock my socks off.
You're more gorgeous than Goldilocks.
You're a cross between Britney, Kylie and Marilyn Monroe.
You're a pearl in the shell,
You're the bell of the ball,
You're my Wonderwall.
You're Supercalifragilisticexpialidocious
And that's hard to say and even harder to spell but I don't care
Because you're my girl and you rock my world.

A ReCiPe FoR DiSaStEr

The other day I decided to bake a mud cake,
With ingredients from the back garden

The recipe goes as follows:

Mud   8oz
Flower buds (As many as you can pick without being
                    Grounded for a week)
Slugs
Bugs 4oz of each
Petals
Stinging nettles (A handful of both)
Ladybirds
Rabbit turds, 2oz of each
Feathers from a number of different variety of garden birds.
A handful of lice.
Any available dead mice.
Rain water (Depending on the weather to bind the
                    Ingredients together)

Then cook for two hours in the baking sun sprinkle with some
Dead flies and some wood shavings, cut off a slice and give it
To your baby sister and tell her it tastes nice!
And when your baby sister starts to cry and your mother asks
Why run and hide, because your name will almost certainly
Be MUD!!

A BiTiNg ReMaRk

Let me introduce you to the shark,
Its bite is worse than its bark.
It's been dying to meet you, before that it eats you
Well at least that's what I heard it remark!

WiTcHeS iN StiTcHeS

Witches can really have me in stitches
Especially when they fall off their broomsticks
Into ditches.
Unfortunately for the witches when they do
They have themselves in stitches too!
(May I suggest the witches try a little witch hazel!)

NoThiNg SnOrEs LoUdEr
ThAn A DiNoSaUr SnOrEs

I'm sure nothing snores louder than a dinosaur snores when a
Dinosaur snores while it's sleeping by the sea shore.

Now say this tongue twisting rhyme fast four times without
Tripping over your tongue.
If you fail, then I'm going to give you a hundred lines on why
You shouldn't fiddle with your mother's kitchen blinds
And then get you to write a tongue twisting rhyme.
Okay, off you go, there's no need to be shy don't worry if you
Make a mistake, I wasn't being unkind, I don't really mind,
I only said that about the hundred lines so the rhyme rhymed!
Okay, so you just about managed to get your tongue round that
One so let's try another one.

> Nothing makes more of a hullabaloo
> Than a kangaroo who's trying to play a didgeridoo
> At a didgeridoo do in Timbucktu at two thirty two.

Over to you!!
What cat got your tongue, have you suddenly been
Struck dumb?
Oh, well it's only a bit of fun.
Try writing your own tongue twisters at school, then
Swap them with your classmates and get your teacher
To write one too that should definitely cause a hullabaloo!
Yes, as they get dafter and dafter and you read them faster
And faster your class mates will end up howling with laughter!
(if you're lucky if not then I'd probably sue!)

CaN YoU Do An AnAgRaM
(Of CoUrSe YoU CaN)

Can you do an anagram? I'm sure you can
Well if you can see how many words
You can make from the word anagram.

If you're not sure what an anagram is
An anagram is a word or phrase made by rearranging the letters
Of another word or phrase.

i.e. Spam - Maps - Amps. Short words are pretty easy but the
Longer they are the harder they get!

Why not do an anagram of your favourite country or band or
An animal or maybe your favourite football team.

Nasty ringtone Cal C. (Accrington Stanley!)
You think you can do better well be my guest!!

Why not try Hamilton Academicals or Annan Athletics
Can you do an anagram? Of course you can.

CoNtrOL FrEaK

I am a big control freak,
I like things nice and neat.
I always like things my own way,
So please do as I say.

I am a big control freak
I know I'm quite abrupt.
And now it's time for me to speak
So please don't interrupt.

I am a big control freak
So please don't break my rules.
I never say things tongue in cheek
And never suffer fools.

I am a big control freak
I weigh up the pros and cons.
I never make a song and dance
And I'm never in the wrong.

I am a big control freak
I'm never meek and mild.
I think I was a control freak
Even as a child.

I am a big control freak
I'm always in the right.
I even control my dreams
When I'm asleep at night!

WhAt'S A PoEm ?

What's a poem? A page full of words,
Jumbled up images some sublime some absurd,
Often never to be read or heard.
Left gathering dust or like some piece of decaying rusty metal
Or windswept rose petals that never settle anywhere.
Words like stinging nettles meant to hurt,
Like dirt, like mud which sticks, and sticks and stones will
Break my bones all recorded on a mobile phone.
All so much hot air but does anybody really care.
All the fun of the funfair. Idle chatter but does it matter?
Platitudes, my ever changing moods, food for thought,
Junk mail, stale words given away at a bring and buy sale.
Just another fairy tale. Poetry's not easy, poetry's hard
Like the Bard waiting to catch you off guard.
A turn of phrase as you turn the page,
Then a shaft of sun light breaks through the clouds,
Some small insight into what the poet writes.
Midsummer night dreams, so serene, sight unseen
Come before they've been.
Words come with surprise as they hit you right between
The eyes, some truth some lies,
A word from the wise in some clever guise
Or other for a mother father sister or brother,
There to discover one throw away line after another.
What is a poem? A page full of words
Some sublime some absurd all longing to be read or heard.

I'M TrYiNg tO WriTe A PoEm AbOuT QuAnTuM MeChAniCs

I'm trying to write a poem about Quantum Mechanics
And I'm not leaving the room until I do.
I'm trying to write a poem about Quantum Mechanics
But I think I've got more chance of jumping over the moon.
I'm trying to write a poem about Quantum Mechanics
Perhaps it would help if I could think outside the box.
I'm trying to write a poem about Quantum Mechanics
But up to this point the whole things got me foxed.
I'm trying to write a poem about Quantum Mechanics
But so far what I've got doesn't make much sense.
I'm trying to write a poem about Quantum Mechanics
But unfortunately like a black hole I think I'm just too dense.
I'm trying to write a poem about Quantum Mechanics
But on the subject I'm not that well read
I'm trying to write a poem about Quantum Mechanics
Perhaps I should get Stephen Hawking to write it instead!

EpiTaPh FoR AuNtiE DoT

Here lies Auntie Dot,
To all of us she meant a lot.
Dead, but not forgotten,
Still tending her forget-me-nots
Here in the family plot.

ReAp WhAt We SoW

We shouldn't complain about the rain
We shouldn't complain about the heat
For without the rain and without the heat
The seeds and wheat would not grow
And we would not reap what we sow.

NoT SuCh WiZaRdS WiTh WoRdS

It happened at the wizards' spelling bee, all the wizards were
Spelling atrociously – well they were trying to, but they kept
leaving the T out or putting Es in where they weren't
Suppose to be.
Yes, I think it's fair to say, it was all going disastrously,
When the head wizard, who was almost lost for words, said
'You're spelling so badly I'm going to have to ex-spell the lot
Of you and ask you to leave.'
Luckily in the nick of time (and for the purpose of this rhyme)
A young wizard by the name of Harry (admittedly not a great
Name for a wizard, but what the hell?) cast a wizard of a spell.
So magnificently, wizardly was it, it made the wizards spell
Perfectly. In fact it was such a wizard of a spell that in the
future Wizards from far and wide would be heard to say 'That Harry,
What a wizard with words!' but when the spell wore off,
The head wizard, a chap by the name of Merlin (now there's
A name for a wizard) when he heard that Harry was being
Called a wizard with words said 'I've never heard anything so
Absurd, Harry a wizard with words he should hang his head in
Shame he can barely spell his own name!'
And on the subject of the wizards' spelling bee Merlin had the
Final word and said now all you wizards can disappear for tea!

AN INTERVIEW WITH A VAMPIRE

Favourite Sport: Any blood sport.

Favourite Drink: Bloody Mary.

Favourite Band: Vampire Weekend & Simply Red

Favourite T.V.   *True Blood*. Anything really as long as it isn't *Buffy the Vampire Slayer*!

Favourite Films: *Interview with the Vampire* & *Twilight*.

Favourite Musical: Blood Brothers.

Favourite Food: Black pudding.

Favourite Country: Rumania.

Favourite place: Transylvania.

Favourite wine: Any good Rumanian red I'm not that fussy.

Favourite song: *Blood on the Dance Floor*
                     Michael Jackson.

Favourite saying: BITE ME!!

Least favourite things: Going to the dentists – it SUCKS!
                         And giving blood it's very draining!!

A PoEm ThAt DoEsN't RhYmE

A poem that doesn't rhyme
Is not a proper poem to my mind.
If it rhymes by accident or design
I don't really mind as long as it rhymes (well most of the time)

It doesn't matter how you make the poem rhyme
Even if you have to include a line like
Rosemary Parsley and Thyme.
Yes, it need not have reason as long as it has rhyme.

Poets these days are more inclined
Not to have their poems rhyme,
And rhyming poetry seems to be on the decline
Which for a rhyming poet is not a good sign.

Struggling for words to rhyme
Why not try the words Greenwich Mean Time,
Or perhaps the word Pantomime,
But try not to be too asinine
Oh, and don't forget the punch line (and you'll be just fine.)

To me a poem that doesn't rhyme is a crime
And the perpetrator of said crime should do time
Yes, that would be poetic justice I think you'll find
And not a bad line on which to end this rhyme.
(After all if you don't want to do the time
  Then you'd better be prepared to do the rhyme!)

My ToOtH JuSt ReAlLy HuRtS LiKe HelL

My tooth just really hurts like hell,
I think I'm going to YELL and YELL.
So pull it out and please be quick,
Because frankly I really feel quite sick.

My tooth just really hurts like hell,
I'm really not feeling very well.
I know it's just a silly fear,
For to the dentists, I haven't been for years.

My tooth just really hurts like hell,
But now it's out you'd never tell.
And all that fuss they say I made,
Well actually I thought I was very brave.

My tooth just really hurts like hell.
Well, actually it doesn't anymore,
Although it is a little sore.
The worst is over of that I'm sure,
And I'll be back in another ten years or more!

The Dentists' Tarter (sorry I mean charter)
I swear to pull the tooth the whole tooth
And nothing but the tooth
So help me Dracula's aunt Ruth
(The one who uses Bluetooth!)

114

WhAtEvEr HaPpEnEd tO tHe WaGoN WhEeL?

I know it might not be any big deal but
Whatever happened to the Wagon Wheel ?
It used to be as big as the moon
Or at least as big as my baby brother's bedroom.
Yes, it used to be cool and as big as a football
Or at least it looked that size on the shelf
Or perhaps I'm just kidding myself.
I swear when I was growing up it was as big as the F.A. Cup
Yes I know it might not be any big deal
But whatever happened to the Wagon Wheel ?
Now some people give you all that spiel that you're looking
Through rose tinted glasses but I'm sure Wagon Wheels
Used to be as big as the sun or at the very least as big as
A giants meal for one.
And I don't care what anyone says I feel I've been done
And although I might say this a little tongue in cheek
But a Wagon Wheel used to keep me going for a whole week!
Personally speaking I think as soon as it became fashionable
To dunk, the Wagon Wheel was sunk (Yes how can you sup
With a Wagon Wheel stuck in your cup!)
Yes, back in the bygone days of chewy comestibles perhaps
Now I really am looking through rose coloured spectacles,
And so to the makers of the Wagon Wheel a word to the wise,
If you don't want to make a grown man cry,
I say with a heavy sigh
Please return my Wagon Wheel back to its original size!

CaLLiGraPHy

Calligraphy I may well have to concede,
However pleasing you are on the eye,
Sometimes you are a little difficult to read!

A FaiRy TaLe

Hans Christian Andersen to his mother
Once (upon a time) said,
Just before she tucked him into bed.
If I became a famous writer
What a fairy tale that would be!

WalLy tHe WoMbAt (WoN't Sit StiLL)

Wally the Wombat won't sit still.
Even when it's ill it won't sit still.
Even when it's climbed to the top of a very steep hill,
It won't sit still.
Even when it's staring at a windmill, it won't sit still.
Even when it gets the bill in a fancy restaurant,
It won't sit still, perhaps it left its gold card on the window sill
Before it left the house (would you credit it!)
Even when it's on a roller coaster ride and it's getting a big
thrill it won't sit still (no wonder it's feeling ill).
Even when it's watching *Neighbours* with its Aunt Lill
And Uncle Phil it won't sit still.
Even when its taken an indigestion pill it won't sit still.
Perhaps it ate a dodgy mixed grill and is feeling a little
Green around the gills.
Even when it's being tranquil it won't sit still.
Even when it's standing still it won't sit still.
Even when it's writing a letter with ink and quill
It won't sit still.
Even when it's watching a boring nil-nil draw between
Melbourne and Sydney it won't sit still.
Even when its asleep it won't sit still.
Even when it's chatting to a duck-billed platypus,
The one with the great big bill, it won't sit still.
Even when it's on a long flight to Brazil it won't sit still.

Continued over the page:

Even when it's got time to kill it won't sit still.
Even when playing a game of chess with a crocodile
Called Will it won't sit still. (Well if it did it would be a dill!)
Even when it gets caught with its hand in the till
And is getting chased by the old bill it won't sit still.
Even when it's at the Sydney Opera House listening to a
Soprano who's voice is shrill it won't sit still.
Why won't Wally the Wombat sit still?
Please tell me, because I think I've had my fill of why Wally
The Wombat won't sit still and frankly it's making me ill!
Well maybe Wally the Wombat is in some sort of trance
Or perhaps it's got St. Vitus dance.
Well, actually, it's none of the above.
The reason Wally the Wombat won't sit still is because
Wally the Wombat has got ants in his pants literally.
Well, that's what happens when you sit on an ant hill,
You wally, Wally!
And that's why Wally the Wombat won't sit still.
Well would you sit still if you had ants in your pants?
No thanks, smarty pants!!

Not So Easily Spooked

The Spook said to the Ghost,
Tongue in cheek, 'Are you alright
Because you look as white as a sheet?'
The Ghost replied, 'I can see right through you,
You're talking complete gobbledegook.
I'm not that easily spooked.'

The Spook said to the Poltergeist,
Tongue in cheek, 'Are you alright
Because you look as white as a sheet?'
The Poltergeist replied, 'That's not very nice.
Are you trying to give me a fright?
Now I'll be up half the night worrying and getting uptight.'

The Spook said to the Vampire,
Tongue in cheek, 'Are you alright
Because you look as white as a sheet?'
The Vampire replied, and in a slightly sarcastic tone,
Said 'Bite me and talk about the pot calling the kettle black,
Have you looked in the mirror lately you look in
A terrible state?
Now I suggest you leave before it's too bloody late.'
And as a parting shot the Vampire said to the Spook
'YOU SUCK' and then disappeared into the night to try his
luck.

Continued over the page:

The Spook said to the Ghoul,
Tongue in cheek, 'Are you alright
Because you look as white as a sheet?'
The Ghoul replied, 'When you said that I nearly died,
But you won't pull the wool over my eyes with that old line
I'm nobody's fool I feel fine.'

The Spook said to the Spirit, tongue in cheek,
'Are you alright because you look as white as a sheet?'
The Spirit turned the other cheek and replied
'I'm not going to sink to your level,' and calmly poured out
A drink of Vodka for his old friend the Devil,
The Spook having seen the devil,
No longer tongue in cheek but extremely mild and meek,
Went as white as a sheet especially when the Devil
Turned up the heat.

And the moral of this devilishly spooky tale
One I've been dying to tell you for weeks
Is if you're a Spook always speak the truth never lie
Or you may well find yourself in hell not feeling very well
Waving your own tail goodbye.

Mind you if you're a Spook I'd probably have to say
That ship has all ready sailed!

A BiT Of A PiCkLe

Pippa Nickle was a bit of a pickle.
She used to ride up and down the street on her bicycle,
Ringing her bell, and creating merry hell.
Either that, or tickling her grandad's feet whilst he was
Trying to get off to sleep.
Not only was Pippa Nickle a bit of a pickle but Pippa Nickle
Was also extremely fickle.
She'd cast her friends aside at the drop of a hat and happily
Rat on them behind their backs.
Pippa Nickle also loved to chase the neighbour's cat around
The garden with a cricket bat. The little brat.
Not too surprisingly the neighbour's cat got a little fed up with
that and one day decided to set a trap for Pippa Nickle to get
his own back.
And when Pippa Nickle caught up with the neighbour's cat,
With a cricket bat, she was pounced on by all the
neighbourhood cats and after that for Pippa Nickle that I'm
afraid was that and nobody ever heard a peep out of Pippa
Nickle ever again and that's a fact!

WhAt A PaNtOMiMe

What a Pantomime and Hullabaloo kids make,
When trying to get out of going to school.
Oh no they don't (Kids say).
Oh yes they do (Parents say).
Just look behind you,
They're hiding in the bathroom pretending to go to the loo
(Which parents always Pooh Pooh!).
They can't find one of their shoes.
(Which creates quite a Bally Hoo!).
They tell you they've got the flu, (Atishyooooo!)
Or they've hurt their leg falling off the kitchen stool
And can't walk to school (Ouch Ooh Boo Hoo Hoo!).
Yes kids make such a Pantomime and Hullabaloo,
As a rule, when trying to get out of going to school.
Oh no they don't!
Oh yes they do! oh yes they do! oh yes they do!
Just look behind you!!!!

DySLeXiA ReAd 'Em AnD WeEp (DYSLEXIA)

Words jump around the page get me in a rage

Why can't they keep still. Words are making me ill.

Ds look like Bs, Bs look like Ds words and letters

Have got me metaphorically on my knees.

One line merges into another I'm not clever like my brother.

Words are making me feel like I'm sea sick and it's beginning
To get on my wick.

Look don't panic it may well be that you're dyslexic

It's no disgrace there's no need to get Sherlock Holmes
On the case. No one's perfect in the human race.

Tell some one close, a friend, a sister, a brother, a father or a
Mother, or a teacher or someone you trust before your head
Goes bust.

A lot of famous people have got dyslexia and believe you me
It's never stopped them succeed.

Beat dyslexia and don't let it stop you in your quest to read.

LiFe's A BeAcH

I love the sun upon my skin.
I love the sea I paddle in.
I love the breeze, I love the shade.
I love the ice creams and lemonade.
I love the castles that I have made.
I love the waves when they misbehave.
I love the cries the seagulls make.
I love the beach I want to stay.

I hate the sea 'coz it's too cold.
I hate the noisy beach patrols.
I hate the sound of all the gulls.
I hate the gaudy parasols.
I hate the wind, when it starts to blow.
I hate the beach, I can't wait to go!

ThAt'S A GoOd FeeD (SoRrY I MeAn ReAd!)

Blood Sports Suck & Count Your Blessings
By I.M. Dracula.

A Lion's Feast By A.J. Wildebeest.

How to Wrestle an Alligator By Will U. Neverlearn.

How to fight off a Great White Shark By Yule B. Lucky.

5O Great Places to Eat. By I.M.A.Vampire.(They all SUCK!)

25 Ways to Cook a Crocodile By Allie Gladiator.

Beware of the Big Bad Wolf By Virginia Riding-Hood

Howling at the Moon by U.R. Changing.

Too Many Cooks Never Spoil the Broth (As Long as they're Cooked Properly) By A. Cannibal.

So Long and Thanks for all the Raw Fish By A.C. Lion.

1O1 Goat Recipes By R.U. Kidding.

All these titles and more available from Bad Books Dot. Con

ExCuSe tHe PuN 3 (ThE UnAbRiDgEd VeRsiOn)

Excuse the pun, but if the Devil's number is 666
Then surely 333 is the number of the Devil's son,
And if you put the two numbers together for a bit of fun
Then you'd get the number 999 which if you met the Devil
And his son you'd want to ring in a hurry or run!
If you then added 666 (18) to 333 (9) you'd get the
Number 27, which coincidentally rhymes with Heaven,
When all's said and done, one place you probably won't
Be going to if you met the Devil and his son!

The author issues a full apology for the rhyme
Excuse the pun 3,
He said sorry, but the Devil just got the better of me!

I just hope I don't get any emails from any religious
Zealots, after all this is a book of nonsense rhymes not the
Satanic Verses!!

WhAt'S So FriGhTeNiNg AbOuT A MeRe CAt?

What's so frightening about a mere cat
After all it's not as if it's a bloodsucking bat
Or a large dirty filthy rat it's only a mere cat.
Yes ha ha, very funny, but have you ever stroked
A meerkat's tummy?
Yes I thought that would get you into a flap
So you'd better scratch that line,
What's so frightening about a mere cat
And get back to writing rhymes about hats or bats
Before that meerkat turns around and attacks
And then you'll find out
What's so frightening about a mere cat!

Yes, I think you need to ensure that no meerkats
Attack mere cats do you understand that......simples!!

A TeEnAgEr'S BeDrOoM

A teenager's room is full of clutter,
Like mobile phones and dirty clothes,
And cd racks and small backpacks,
And magazines and computer games and growing pains
But rarely ever lets in the rain,
Unless of course there's a hurricane.

A teenager's room is very cool
And free from school it has no rules.
It's full of smiles and little white lies
And hormones that are in overdrive,
It contains tears a million hopes and fears
And even the odd can of beer!

A teenager's room is a magic place with little space
Because of all the junk they simply cannot throw away,
And schemes and dreams and tearful scenes
Some played out on a computer screen.

A teenager's room conceals broken hearts
And quite loud farts, (mostly from the boys!)
A million laughs,
A portable TV some mobiles hanging from the ceiling
And a diary kept well out of sight
So mums and dads cannot pry.

Continued over the page :

A teenager's room is a sanctuary of sorts.
A place to work, a place to rest.
It's the worst, it's the best,
It's better than all the rest.
It's chocked full of soaps, jokes books and clocks
And it definitely rocks
(Although sometimes parents wish it didn't!)
The only time it gets cleaned is when Mum and Dad
Take a hoover to it but it doesn't stay that way for long
Unless, pocket money is involved.
Then as if by magic it's as clean as a whistle in ten minutes flat
But with all that clutter if you believe that you'll believe
Anything and that's a fact!

Anyway we were all teenagers once.
Less we forget, which we often do.
So we shouldn't be to quick to judge
Just give 'em enough love and hugs to get them through
Yes that'll do cool!

Like A Snowflake

Surely there can be no mistake
That we're all unique like a snowflake
Falling gently upon a frozen lake.
We give we take we bend we break.
Our fate, like a snowflake to evaporate
As it slowly disappears before our eyes.
We too have to say goodbye.
Sometimes we look to the sky and ask why
But there's no reply,
Just the sound of the wind rustling through the trees
As it sheds its leaves.
Some believe the reply comes when the end is nigh,
Silently coming like a spirit in the night,
A bright guiding light to take us to the other side.
Some believe with a gentle sigh that this is all there is,
But the enquiring mind still asks why.
Does our soul disappear like the fallen snow
Or does it like a seed re-grow.
Is it all on the simple throw of a dice
Or is it the divine hand of our maker.
Until we get to the other side (if there is one)
Only you can decide.

130

HeRoEs

Heroes are my heroes like Jimmy Dean
And Steve McQueen, and all the astronauts on Apollo 13.
Che Guevara, Bruce Lee and fireman and women
Wherever they maybe.
Elvis and Eddie Cochran too
Bo Diddley who played the blues.
Batman and Robin and the Fantastic Four,
Judge Dredd – I Am the Law,
And the American rapper 2Pac Shakur.
Whoever created ice cream cones,
And down loading the Heroes ringtone to my mobile phone.
Neil Armstrong the first man on the moon.
Marilyn Monroe who still makes me swoon.
Jimi Hendricks and Marvin Gaye,
Bob Geldof and Billie Holiday.
Yuri Gagarin the first man in space,
Sherlock Holmes who's always on the case.
Barack Obama, The Dali Lama
The writers of the drama Futurama.
Heroes by David Bowie
Nelson Mandela too
Joseph Heller the man who wrote the novel Catch 22
No more Heroes by the Stranglers will do
Those are my heroes how about you?

A VAMPIRES PLIGHT

A VAMPIRE SUCKS,
A VAMPIRE BITES,
A VAMPIRE LOOKS AN AWFUL SIGHT.
ESPECIALLY IN THE MORNING LIGHT,
AFTER HE'S BEEN UP HALF THE NIGHT
SUCKING AND BITING, WELL SERVES HIM RIGHT!
WELL, LET'S FACE IT, VAMPIRES AREN'T TOO
BRIGHT.
THOUGH MAYBE THAT'S BECAUSE
THEY'RE ALREADY DEAD AND HAVEN'T GOT
ONE SINGLE BRAIN CELL IN THEIR POOR LITTLE
HEADS.
YES, IT'S A VAMPIRE'S PLIGHT TO ROAM THE
EARTH
EVERY NIGHT OR UNTIL A VAMPIRE SLAYER
 (POSSIBLY BUFFY) DECIDES OTHERWISE,
WATCH OUT SPIKE!
AND THE VAMPIRE'S FROM TWILIGHT!!

WhEn VaMPiReS GeT PaNgS ThEn OuT CoMe
ThEiR FaNgS!!

EvErYbOdY NeEdS A HuG

As you stand there and shrug remember
Everybody needs a hug

With a hug you feel loved

Without a hug you feel as small as a bug

With love you feel missed

Without love you feel you don't exist

With an embrace you feel like part of the human race

Without an embrace you feel like you've fallen down
A Black hole in outer space.

As you stand there and shrug remember
Everybody needs a hug

WaNnAbE

I'm a legend in my own lunch time
The original wannabe
The only person I've got time for
Is me, me, me, me, me!

TwiNkLe TwiNkLe LiTtLe SaTeLliTe

Twinkle, twinkle little star
How I wonder what you are
Or perhaps you're not a star at all
But just a satellite that's very small!

YoUR WoRsT NiGhTmArE

Spider, spider, on the stairs
Are you sitting there for a dare?
Or is it that you just don't care?
Either way you'd better beware,
For here I come your worst nightmare.
There, now you're dead,
Squashed on the bottom of my shoe
Well to be fair Mr Spider I did try and warn you!

ApRiL FoOL

Hasn't anybody told you it's not cool
To be an April fool?
So a word to the wise,
Don't let some fool catch you by surprise
And pull the wool over your eyes!

NeVeR QuEsTiOn A CoBrA SnAkE

Never question a Cobra Snake
for to do so would be a grave mistake!

I CoULdN't CaRe LeSs

My rooms a mess and I couldn't care less.
I can't be bothered to get dressed and I couldn't care less.

My little brother Seth has just beaten me at chess,
And I couldn't care less.

The cat's got its head stuck in the trouser press
And I couldn't care less.

My mum's just given up smoking and she's very stressed
And I couldn't care less.

Apparently, someone hid my grandad's false teeth in the
Compost heap, though who is anybodies guess,
And I couldn't care less.

My older sister Tess has just failed her driving test
And I couldn't care less.

Today they officially called off the search for the Loch Ness
Monster, and I couldn't care less.

I recently sent for a book off the internet called *The Power
Of Positive Thinking* which is taking so long to get to me I
Think they must have sent it by pony express!
And still I couldn't care less.
'Mum, why is my tea not on the table and why is that TV
Repair man taking the TV out the door?'
Now I must confess I've never cared more!

ThE OcELoT

Not a lot rhymes with ocelot
Apart from the words shot, rot, hot, pot, clot and jot
So I shot the rotten ocelot and put it in a hotpot then
Ate it for my tea.
Well, you tell me who gives a jot about the ocelot, not me!
Look you clot have you lost the plot,
I didn't really shoot the ocelot it's just a nonsense rhyme
I'd never be that unkind.
Anyway I wouldn't even know how to cook an ocelot.
By the way, is ocelots the right term for a lot of ocelot or not?

CaN YoU KeEp A SeCrEt ?

Can you keep a secret? No, not me!
I'm a goose and my lips are loose.
You'd be better off telling your secret
To a hippopotamus or a flea,
Than telling it to me.

Can you keep a secret? No, not me!
I'm a parrot and I just talk and talk incessantly.
Can't you see you'd be better off telling your secret
To a tiger or a bee than telling it to me.

Can you keep a secret? No, not me!
I'm a rabbit and I just rabbit on and on and on,
You'd be better off telling your secret
To a grizzly bear I swear or a kiwi
Than telling it to me.

Can you keep a secret? No, not me!
I'm a yak and all I do all day long is
Yakkety yak as all us yaks do.
You'd be better off telling your secret to a gnu
Or a fish that lives in the sea,
Than telling it to me.
Now please leave me be.

Continued over the page:

Can you keep a secret? Yes, I can!
I'm a wise old owl and I'll never create a row
I'll be more than happy to keep your secret
If you tell me, well for a small fee,
Oh by the way what is your secret?
Oh I see, you're a rhinoceros that thinks it's a flea
Well that's preposterous and almost impossible to believe,
But don't worry your secrets safe with me,
Now would you like a nice cup of herbal tea?

FoOtBalL KeNniNg (FiRsT HaLf)

Flag waving,
Penalty saving,
Fans wailing,
Managers raving,
Referee's eyesight failing,
Players badly behaving.
Goalkeepers flailing,
At half time your team one-nil trailing.
The ball over the bar goes sailing.
The fourth official hailing.
Prima donna's hair braiding,
Players on relegated teams bailing.
Trophy's engraving.
Old players stories regailing.
Statues of famous players unveiling,
Floodlights failing,
But always the beautiful game prevailing.

DoN't LeT tHe BeD BuGs BiTe

One day a bug got into a fight with a slug.
The bug, who it has to be said was a bit of a thug,
Said to the slug, you bug me, and proceeded to slug the bug,
Though why the bug was bugged by the slug, I'm not too sure.
The slug simply shrugged and told the bug he had an ugly mug
and that the bug bugged him too and proceeded to slug
The bug back. (I hope your keeping up with all this!)
The bug then fell to the floor and the bug was no more.
You could say the slug pulled the rug from underneath the
Bugs feet if you like either way, it wasn't much of a fight.
Anyway, sleep tight, oh and don't let the bed bugs bite alright!

JeEpErS CrEePeRs

Jeepers creepers rhinos are heavy sleepers
And once they've fallen asleep on the floor
You won't get a peep out of them that's for sure
That's until they start to snore
Then jeepers creepers those rhinos are impossible to ignore!

MeOW !

Cats are just so selfish
It's all me(ow) me(ow) me(ow) me(ow) Meow!

143

ThiNgS I'd LiKe tO ThRoW iNtO A BLaCk HoLe

Maths, Junk mail, DIY Addicts & Country & Western tapes.

Nightmares, Dentist chairs, Daddy-long-legs & All Loos at
Rock Festivals too. Gorgonzola cheese, Lawyers fees, air
Conditioning on planes & Acid rain.

Loud farts, Early morning starts, Clowns on unicycles and Cars
That belch black smoke would all get my vote.

Exams, Spam (both types) All rap videos and Black holes!

Colds, Liver & Bacon casseroles, Know-it-alls & Loo rolls.

Rules, Shopping malls, Toothache & Marzipan Xmas Cakes.

Homework, Red tape, Call centres & the P.C. Brigade.

Fights, luddites, sounds bites, flickering lights, & people who
Abuse other people's human rights.

Peas, Fleas, & 8O% of reality TV.
Bee hives, Wide ties, Footballers who dive & Goodbyes.

Guns, Currant buns, and Xmas number 1s.

Clogs, Rubbish Snogs, and loud annoying barking Dogs.
SATS, Rats, hissing Cats and Moles Yes, all of these things
And more I'd like to throw into a Black Hole!

ScArEdY-CAt

My cat is scared of mice and rats,
She is a big fat scaredy-cat.
She's scared of mobile phones that ring,
And birds that tweet and birds that sing.
She's even scared of my nephew's bling,
In fact she's scared of everything.

She even gets a fright at night
The minute that I turn out the light.
It doesn't seem to me quite right,
She's scared of everything in sight.

She's like a cat on a hot tin roof
That's how she is when she gets spooked.
She even scares herself at times
This big fat scaredy-cat of mine.

Her nerves have got so bad in fact
I'm now giving Prozac to my scaredy-cat.
So now she lies upon the mat
With a grin as wide as a Cheshire cat!

ViTaMiN ViTaLiTy FrOm A tO Z

I have to take my vitamin pills,
Because they are the answer to all my ills.
Big ones,
Small ones,
All sizes and shapes,
Just one a day I'm suppose to take.
But I have Iron,
Vitamin C, Zinc,
Selenium and Omega 3s,
Vitamin D,
Vitamin E,
Vitamin A to Vitamin Z.
I think it's pretty plain to see
One vitamin's not enough for me.
Well why take one when you can take twenty three?

ThE BeE's KnEeS

I agree a killer bee
Might not be everybody's cup of tea
But to another killer bee
A killer bee really is the bee's knees!

ThE JoKe'S On YoU

The joke's on you.
Well, it is if you're wearing a shirt that looks
Like an explosion in a paint factory.
One you'd only wear if you were holidaying
In Honolulu,
Or you're wearing a garish tie a mile wide
Or you're a clown wearing great big floppy shoes.
Yes, then the joke's definitely on you!

My ImAgiNAtiOn'S RuNniNg WiLd

Like an excited child my imagination was running wild.
So I thought I'd better rein it in before my wild imagination
Got the better of me and was captured and put in a cage and I
Was told to act my age.
But as I turned the page my imagination went into a rage.
It had no intention of being caught restrained and put into a
cage so I read on, my imagination now running wild and free,
Rampaging ferociously like a hungry animal gobbling up the
words in front of me.
So they sent the hunters out with guns and spears and set down
Traps to stop my imagination in its tracks,
But my imagination wasn't going to give up without a fight,
Like some poor wild unsuspecting boar.
So my imagination roared then soared like some majestic
Flying dinosaur and by the time I'd reached chapter four
The hunters of my imagination were no more.

CaPtAinS BLoG StAr DaTe 2OO8
(A BaD DaY At WoRk FoR A TReKkiE)

I got up at a quarter to eight, was in a bit of a state
Because I was running late.
Knew I'd be in for some flack but you cannot change
The laws of physics Capt. and that's a fact.
By midday I was all behind, having a bad day,
I think it's fair to say, dealing with the Ferengay.
At one, on the run, got a quick bite a Danish pastry with a
Cup of coffee already felt like saying "Beam me up Scottie".
By three I was making up for lost time,
Couldn't even stop for a cup of tea.
By four I was on the shop floor,
Boldly going where no man has gone before.
By five working at warp drive I was barely alive, though I
don't know how, fighting Klingons off the starboard bow.
By six was still in a fix, needed Mr Spock the one with
The pointy ears to make all this work disappear.
By seven I had finally finished for the day – Hooray!
No more work, went home for some tea, watched a *Star Trek*
Dvd featuring Capt. James T. Kirk.
After a day of hurly burly went to bed early,
Because as they say, early to bed early to rise,
For another hectic day on the Star Ship Enterprise.
Dealing with people who are surly
And a complete waste of space,
For another long day dealing with the human race!

SPikE AnD HiS SiStEr'S BrIgHt PiNk BiKe

Poor old Spike was forced to ride his sister's bright pink bike
Which got poor old Spike into nothing but trouble and strife
Getting him into fights making him up tight and keeping him
Awake half the night.
Poor old Spike felt it just wasn't right that he had to ride his
Sister's bright pink bike but his parents just couldn't afford a
New bike for Spike and Spike knew his parents were just trying
To be kind and it was just unfortunate they happened to be
Colour blind so poor old Spike pretended he didn't really mind.
Yes, poor old Spike would rather be doing anything than
having to ride his sister's bright pink bike like flying his kite
Or hiking up to Devil's Dyke or fishing with his best friend
Mike and catching a record-sized pike anything as long as he
didn't have to ride his sister's bright pink bike.
The only time that Spike didn't mind riding his sister's bright
Pink bike was at night, when everyone was well out of sight.
Poor old Spike longed for some respite from having to ride
His sister's bright pink bike, and every time he went to the
Shops he would leave his sister's bright pink bike outside
Hoping some kind person would steal it,
But it was bright pink and when Spike came out of the shops
It would always still be standing there and poor old Spike's
Heart would sink.
It got so bad Spike even considered breaking his ankle on an
Ice rink yes Spike's sister's bright pink bike was driving poor
Old Spike to drink.

Continued over the page:

Then one day when Spike had gone out on his sister's
Bright pink bike he saw a girl on a bright pink bike
For Spike it was love at first sight.
The girl saw Spike riding his sister's bright pink bike
And although nothing was said the girl went bright red.
Both Spike and the girl then rode off side by side
And ever since that day Spike has permanently been in
The pink along with his friend Lily.
Yes I know that sounds silly................................
But not as silly as you might think!

There's a song called *Lily the Pink*
Which was a number one record by the group The Scaffold.
(Remember records, big black plastic things with a hole in
  the middle?)
  Well download it then, I'm sure it's on the information
  Superhighway somewhere!!

151

ThE DaY ThE SeTtEe SwAlLoWeD GrAnDaD

One day Grandad was happily sitting on the settee
Sipping his tea and eating biscuits from the biscuit tin
When the settee gave a great big grin and invited grandad in.
The settee burped and said 'Pardon me!'
We only found Grandad, or what was left of him,
His false teeth, braces and knobbly knees,
When dad was searching for his lost car keys down the back
Of the settee, along with a couple of dvds and the remote
Control for the TV.
Later we laid a wreath at the foot of the settee and as a mark
Of respect for Grandad didn't sit on the settee for a week.
My dad loved the old settee as he said it was so comfortable,
So despite the fact that the settee had swallowed Grandad,
He was loathed to get rid of it but warned the settee that if it
Ever swallowed or bit anyone in the future he'd personally
Skip it and then later take it down the local tip.
The settee apologised profusely for swallowing Grandad
And agreed he would never swallow or bite anyone ever again
And he hoped that everyone would forgive him and they could
All get back to being friends.
The moral of this tale which is admittedly a little hard to
swallow is never ever get too comfortable sitting on your settee
Watching TV eating your tea because you never know just how
Hungry your settee maybe!!

(Although I do realise that last suggestion could well lead to
  chronic indigestion!)

ThE MaGiC TrUnK

In my attic there's a trunk
And in it I found a lot of old junk.
A pirate ship that had been sunk,
A spaceship from another galaxy,
Big foot, (That one could be debunked!)
A game of Kirplunk.
An old exam I had flunked.
The Loch Ness monster,
A tee shirt that in the wash had shrunk,
Four days off school I had bunked,
A ghost, a genie's lamp, a penny black stamp,
The Four Musketeers and some sticky yuky green gunk!
Frankenstein's monster,
A wizard's pointy hat.
A thousand noisy bats an old moth eaten toy cat.
A fire eating dragon,
An elephant with an extremely large trunk
A movie star hunk, a singing chipmunk,
A basketball that the Harlem Globetrotters had slam-dunked.
A cyber punk, a pirate that was drunk,
Presumably from the pirate ship that was sunk.
Some of my dad's old albums of jazz funk
An old Presbyterian monk.
I then shut the lid down and it made a loud clunk!
As at this point I heard the phone ring,
Yes a child's imagination is a wonderful thing!

A NoNsEnSe RhYMe WiTh ANiMaLs iN MiNd

I wouldn't mind taking a gander at a goose or a panda
Or even a salamander,
Or take a peek at the feet of a duck-billed platypus
Or a centipede.
Wouldn't it be sublime to dine out with a swine,
Like a pot bellied pig.
Drink some fine wine from a chalice in a palace in Bahrain,
To unwind.
And wouldn't it be cool to have a marmoset as a pet and
Take it to the mall.
Or dash around town with a grey hound,
In your dressing gown on a unicycle dressed as a clown.
Or roll around in a bog with a warthog and then consume
A whole chocolate log and be as sick as a dog or maybe not.
Or maybe dance to the early morning light with a Hippo
-potamus in a night club no surely that would be preposterous.
Or get drunk with a skunk listening to a covers band called the
Boomtown Bats that weren't all that.
Or perhaps take a ride in a sports car with a giraffe for a laugh
Or you could just write a nonsense rhyme with animals in mind
To pass the time!

YoU'Re JuSt A SnAkE iN tHe GrAsS

'You're just a snake in the grass and you're getting under
My skin,' said the snake in the grass to the adder, getting
madder and madder.
'And you're simply poisonous and I've got no problem
Grassing you up.'
'You must be having a laugh you're a pain in the grass,'
Said the adder, 'don't be so daft you're far badder than me
By half,' and the adder had the last laugh when he rattled off
Several more biting remarks, each one a little more biting
Than the last, the last one being 'you're a viper in my bosom.'
The grass snake was aghast and crushed by these rather
salacious remarks.
The adder knew he had the grass snake rattled when the
Grass snake slithered off into the grass with its tail between
Its legs feeling sadder than it had ever felt before, knowing
Full well to the adder he'd lost the debate over who was the
badder snake.
The adder gladder than he had been for quite some time,
Feeling like he'd just won a game of snakes and ladders
Coiled himself around a rake and hissed that grass snake
'Made a big mistake dicing with me, I don't think we'll see
Him again in a hurry.'
The adder then fell into a deep sleep dreaming about a rather
Attractive female anaconda called Rhonda he once met at a
Snakes' convention somewhere near the Great Lakes!

JaCk It iN JaCk
& ThRoW AwAy YoUr BeAnS!

Here's some advice to Jack in *Jack and the Beanstalk*.

1. Don't swap the beans for a cow unless with your
   Mother you want to get into a blazing row.

& 2. When the giant snores, make a beeline for the door,
   And then keep going until you've climbed down the
   Beanstalk and when your feet have touched the floor.
   Then cut down the beanstalk with a chainsaw as by
   This time the giant will be after you of that I'm sure
   Until you hear a giant roar and then the giant will
   Be no more!

   And I know Jack you're not too bright
   But if you take this simple advice you'll be alright
   After all it's not rocket science is it Jack you muppet?
   And they said Humpty Dumpty was a right numpty!!

ThE DrEaM TeAm

This is my dream team
Which I gleaned from a football magazine.

Banks or Van der Sar in goal
Defenders Terry, Ferdinand and Ashley Cole,
Beckenbauer and Bobby Moore
Who'd never let the opposition score.

In midfield I'd have Roy Keane
Because he's really tough and mean
Lampard, Fabregas and Scholes
Of whom would also score you goals.

On the wings,
Mathews on the left and Ronaldo on the right
Which for defenders would be quite a frightening sight.

In attack,
Best, Pele, Charlton, Maradona, Messi and Law
Who would simply score you goals galore.

There is of course just one small hitch
I've got too many players out on the pitch!

Actually there's another hitch to buy this team
I'd have to be very, very, very rich!!

YoU HoRriD CrEaTuRe

You're a Wombat
You're a dirty Rat
You're as blind as a Bat
You're an Ass
You're a Shark
You're a Snake in the grass
You're Fowl
You're a Sow
You're a cow
You big Moose
You silly Goose
You're a Sabre tooth with a screw loose
You're a dumb Ox
You're as sly as a Fox
You're a Pig, you're a Swine
You're asinine
You're as prickly as a Porcupine
You're never happy, you never smile
You're as snappy as a Crocodile
You're just a Minor Bird that runs with the herd
You're a flunkie
You're a little monkey
You're in bad shape you great Ape and I'll go the whole Hog
And say you're nothing but a Hound Dog
You're Cuckoo, you're mad as a March Hare
And you I just can't Grizzly Bear
And I know it sounds like I've got a Bee in my bonnet
But buzz off and leave me be before I think of another
Waspish comment!!

A CoMmOtiOn iN tHe OcEaN

One day (out of the blue) there was a bit of a commotion
In the ocean, where, shockingly, there was a squid digging
An electric eel in the ribs (and I'm not telling fibs!)
An octopus blowing his lid and a stingray trying to get his
Own way, shouting the odds to a poor cod that wasn't that
Happy either. Well, would you be if you were stuck on the
End of a fishing rod? (mind you what a cod is doing in the
Ocean is any one's guess, perhaps it got lost, that cod must be
like a fish out of water still it is a nonsense rhyme so I suppose
The cod didn't mind!)
And a whale was getting the hump over getting the bumps
On his birthday, somewhere near the Bay of Biscay.
A shark was getting extremely narked with a dolphin who
Suggested his bite was worse than his bark, which he thought
Was way off the mark.
A flying fish flew into a rage as a turtle told him to act
His age.
Even the crustaceans were flapping in frustration and hadn't
A clue what to do to improve the situation.
Luckily one of the senior humpback whales had a notion to
Pass a motion that everybody that inhabited the ocean should
Take a potion to calm themselves down so in future,
In the ocean you wouldn't be able to hear a single sound.
This law was duly passed although some fish thought it was a
Little daft and that the law would never last, especially the
Flying fish who as soon as they had heard the law had been
Passed, flew off the handle once again.

Continued over the page:

Ever since then, there has hardly be a commotion in the ocean
Of any kind, well none that readily springs to mind.
And as sharks barely ever show emotion anyway,
For them it wasn't much of a problem and apart from a few
Crabs doing the locomotion and a few humpback whales
Having a whale of a time chasing their own tails and the odd
Dolphin making a slight din, tickling passing swimmers with
Their fins, all was well.
Yes I think it's fair to say that these days a commotion in the
ocean is a fairly rare occurrence and mostly in the ocean it's
All peace love and devotion, now where's that sun tan lotion!

(Mind you recently there has been a bit of a commotion in
The ocean, when rather a lot of oil got spilled where it
Shouldn't have been spilled...... but that's another story!)

160

LaWs FoR BaBy DiNoSaUrS

1. Don't put your claws in the coleslaw.

2. Don't scratch or gnaw on the cave doors.

3. Don't leave your room looking like an eyesore.

4. Don't chase wild bore anywhere near a cliff
   Yes that's one law you should never ignore!

5. Avoid a stegosaurus, the one with the great big jaws!

6. Don't leave your toys on the cave floor so daddy dinosaur
   Can fall over them or there will be hell to pay for sure.

7. When you hear your father snore keep you loud rock
   Music down to a dull roar, especially if you're listening
   To T-Rex, Queens of the Stone Age or Dinosaur Junior.

8. Don't slam the cave doors.

9. No boring jokes about dinosaurs (did he sawus?)
   Yes that one should definitely be against the law!

1O. Don't steal anything from the local convenience store.

Yes these are ten basic laws for baby dinosaurs
Oh, one more law for all dinosaurs that shouldn't be ignored
Avoid being destroyed by a giant rogue asteroid!

TrUe Or FaLsE (ToNgUe iN ChEeK)

There was a young man called Keith
Who owned some remarkable false teeth
When he turned out the light
They'd chatter all night
Which I think you'll agree is unique!
(Well apart from in the rhyme trick or treat!)

Poor old Keith I bet he had trouble getting off to sleep,
But was it true or false or just tongue in cheek
Well it's no good asking me, if you want to know the answer
You'll have to ask Keith!

A TiP FoR GeTtiNg OfF tO SLeEp

Here's a tip for getting off to sleep
If you're going to count sheep don't count sheep
That bleat!

WhO'd Be A ReFeReE ?

Who'd be a referee? Certainly not me
Not for all the tea in China
I'd rather be a bad rock climber
Or work in a greasy American diner
Or be an air steward on a low budget airliner
Or be an old timer
Or be a miner forty-niner
Or be a boxer with a great big shiner
Or be a panto-mimer!
Or a children's rhymer
Or a water diviner
Yes, who'd be a referee nobody if you ask me
Nobody apart from a referee
And we all know most referees
Are one whistle short of a pea!

BeWaRe Of LoW FLyiNg ELePhAnTs
(ArE YoU LiStEniNg DuMbO?)

It has to be said (though I've got no idea why!)
If an elephant fell from the sky
And landed on your head
It really wouldn't matter how big or small the elephant was
Because either way you're gonna end up dead!

ALiEn AbDuCtiOn iN ReVeRsE

Last week I abducted an alien
And took him home for tea.
Well it was better I abducted the alien
Than the alien abducting me!

(Yes, you're right it was E.T. that I abducted
And took home for tea! No, we didn't watch E.T.)
We watched *Mars Attacks* on dvd!!)

164

BiRd BrAiN

Was Icarus simply dumb to fly so close to the sun?
Wasn't he aware that as soon as he got anywhere
Near the sun his wax and feathers would run.
And I bet Icarus weighed a ton
I bet Icarus's father thought here I've produced a
Right one.(twit tu-woo!)
Surely the bird brain must have been insane?
Or perhaps he was just looking for fortune and fame.
And for Icarus to think he was a bird can only be said
to be absurd frankly I don't believe a single word
In conclusion I'd have to say it's a nice story
If a little far fetched but in this day and age I'm
afraid
This story just won't fly!!
(Anymore than an elephant would!)

165

MoNsTeR SaLe

MONSTER SALE

Everything must go

Especially that little MONSTER over there
by the clothes rail picking his nose!!

ThE MeDuSa DeBaTe

They say Medusa's hair was made of snakes.
Well no wonder every time Medusa washed her hair
She got into such a terrible state!
And they said with just one look she could turn you to stone
And often did to anybody with a particularly annoying
Ringtone!

Personally speaking, I think it was a wig made to look
Like snakes, but if it wasn't, sorry Medusa my mistake.
Imagine a hair full of snakes.
I bet Medusa found it hard getting a date.
And here's a thought, do you think Medusa had to comb
Her hair with a rake?
Look give me a break what do I know about Medusa
For heavens' sake?
Mind you I do have some interesting thoughts on
Jason and the Argonauts!!

WhAt A PLaNk!

There was a young man called Hank
Who was forced to walk the plank.
He said with a smile,
'I'll see you all in awhile.'
As the ship he was on slowly sank!

NoT SuCh A PLaNk

There was a young man called Hank
Who was forced to walk the plank.
He said with a smile,
'I'll see you all in awhile.'
As the ship he was on slowly ran aground
Onto a sandbank and then Hank stepped off
Onto the shore then went to the nearest bank
Where he deposited twenty gold doubloons
That he had concealed in his trouser pockets
Before he was forced to walk the plank.
Now who's a plank?
Certainly not Hank!!

WeReWoLf BLuEs

It's not much fun being a werewolf in truth,
Especially when you're getting a little long in the tooth.
With all that biting and howling at the moon,
It's enough to fill an old werewolf with gloom.
Who would I'm sure much rather be tucked up in bed
In a nice warm room along with their long suffering wife
Ruth (I assume!)
Or be a vampire happily sleeping in his tomb.
Than getting into strife with the wife
Or giving some poor passer-by the fright of their life.
Yes it's not much fun being a werewolf in truth that's
Getting a little long in the tooth.
Hanging outside phone booths waiting for unsuspecting
Youth who these days are pretty uncouth and run around
In packs ready to attack at the drop of a hat
A bit like a werewolf you could say in fact.
Yes, it's getting more and more hairy and down right scary
These days dealing with the drunk and leery.
Yes, for an ageing Werewolf who'd much rather be watching
TV and getting merry sipping a glass of sherry than to be out
In all weather fighting through the bracken and heather.
No wonder old werewolves are at the end of their tether.
Yes, it's not much fun being a werewolf in truth,
When you're getting a little long in the tooth!

YoU'Re BeHaViNg LiKe A BuNcH Of ANiMaLs

'I find reptiles quite vile,' said the lizard, with a wry smile,
To the crocodile, while they were both swimming down
The River Nile.

'I don't give a monkeys if you've got flees,' said the sloth
Who was down on his knees for a bit of a wheez,
To the chimpanzee who was swinging through the trees.

'You're just being absurd,' said the elephant when he heard
That the antelope, who was standing on a slippery slope,
Wanted to elope with a minor bird.

'I don't give a rats if it doesn't last,' said the squid for a laugh,
When he was asked about his impending marriage to a
Great white shark.

'You're driving me bats,' said the angry gnu, to the rats who
Were slowly gnawing through the bars at the local zoo
Because they had nothing else to do.

'Yes, you're all behaving like a bunch of animals,' said the
Cannibals to the mammals, who were getting the hump with
A group of dromedary camels.

The author is quite well aware that camels are mammals but
Mammals turn on their own kind all the time, so it makes
perfect sense especially in a nonsense rhyme!

ThE WoOd ChOpPeR MaN

Here comes the wood chopper man, chopper in hand
Chopping off heads as fast as he can.
And it's no good hiding there under the bed, because
That's where the wood chopper man hides all his heads.

1,2,3,4   Look at the heads roll along the floor
          (Yes, it's gory but give us some more.)

5,6,7,8   you'd better run before it's too late
          (And it will be too late if you trip at the gate)

Here comes the wood chopper man, chopper in hand,
Chopping off heads as fast as he can.

8,7,6,5   You're extremely lucky if you're still alive

4,3,2,1   that's it, the wood chopper man's done.

And I'm sorry to spoil your fun but even the wood chopper
man gets tired of chopping off heads and needs to rest his own
Head and go to bed.
After all, it has to be said, that tomorrow the wood chopper
man has a long day ahead of him chopping off heads.
So if you've got any sense, then by tomorrow you will have
Fled or otherwise instead you'll be the wood chopper man's
Next head and you'll be the one seeing red!!

After reading this rhyme please don't watch *Dawn of the Dead*
Before you go to bed watch *Mary Poppins* instead!

CrOsSwOrDs

```
              SPITE            I
      H         E            IRATE
   NARKED     TEMPER           R
      T         V           SNAPPY
      E       VEXED           S
                D            LIVID        F
                              B         FUMING
   WRATH               C     L            R
      E   W         ENRAGED               I
    CASTIGATE          O               ANNOYED
      T   L         TESTY               U
   VILE   D          S                  S
      D
```

I'm so ANGRY that I can't think of any more cross words!
Can you?   If you can could you give me a clue,
If not, then I'm off to do another Sudoku!!

172

YoU'Re A LaUgHiNg StOcK

I don't mean to mock
But when they put your head in the stocks
You won't be laughing then
Definitely not!

ThAt'S No JoKe

That's no joke the yoke cried
to the egg that was being fried!

I'Ve GoT BuTtErFLiEs iN My StOmAcH

I woke up this morning and my stomach felt funny.
It was almost as if I had butterflies in my tummy.
But I thought to myself, *don't be such a dummy,*
How can I have butterflies in my tummy?
I mean how on earth did they get in there in the first place,
Through my mouth while I was asleep or up my nose?
Though how they managed to get up such a small hole,
Heaven only knows.
Or perhaps they crawled in my ears, either way
I wish they'd all just disappear.
So I ran up to my mum and said 'I know this sounds dumb
Mum, but I think I've got butterflies in my tum.'
My mum said 'Don't worry dear I think I can help here
To alleviate your fears and make those butterflies disappear.
Just open up your mouth and shout and I'm sure those
Butterflies will fly right on out.'
So I opened up my mouth and shouted as loud as I could
And as I did the butterflies flew right on out,
Along with a spider and a couple of flies much to my surprise,
Although one or two butterflies flew out of my nose and one
Even landed on my big toe.
And now my stomach feels fine. So it just goes to show,
How much my mother really knows,
And that spelling bee I'm doing at school today,
I'm not even worried about anymore.
In fact I can't wait to go!

SpiDeRs ArE A PeSt

Spiders are insiders and outsiders,
And some hide and some we can't abide.
Some frighten us, some bite us,
And some even have their own website
Which to me doesn't seem quite right.
Some spiders we keep as pets,
And some spiders we detest,
And some spiders are a pest.
Actually all spiders are a pest,
Even the ones we keep as pets!
Some spiders infest our house's with their nests
And some spiders scare us half to death,
Especially when we find them in our beds.
Some spiders are winners and money spinners.
Well, money spiders are or so some people believe.
But I think that's just a web of (f)lies if you ask me.
Some spiders make us run and some spiders
End up in our tum (Yum, Yum!)
And some spiders bite us down under on the bum.
Well, Red backs do when hiding in the outside loo!
And I'm not being funny but in Australia it's called the dunny.
Either way spiders are much more scared of us than we
Are of them, or is that the other way round?
And as we both make a beeline for the door
I'd have to say spiders are a pest that's for sure!!

No NeEd tO GeT CaTtY NoW !

Cats on the prowl stop for a pow wow,
Then it rains and they're treated to a power shower
For their pains,
And we all know how much cats hate the rain,
What a shame ……..MEOW!!

HiStORy YoUr HiStOrY

I know this sounds a little daft
But the trouble with history is it's living in the past.
It should have a complete makeover
And bring itself right up to date
And start looking to the future before it's too late!

ThE StOrY Of tHe InViSiBLe CAt

The good thing about the invisible cat is absolutely nothing
It just lays on the mat getting fat.
At that very moment the invisible cat woke up.
You could see by the expression on its face it was visibly
upset, 'I smell a rat,' said the invisible cat, 'I may well be
Invisible but I'm not deaf and I'm not fat.
As a matter of fact I'm nowhere near as fat as some invisible
Cats I could mention,'
And with that the invisible cat yawned, closed its eyes and laid
back down on the mat.
'Invisible my eye,' muttered the invisible cat, a little indignantly
Under his breath, 'I'm no more invisible than Harvey the
Invisible rabbit,' he said as he fell into a purr-fect dream,
Like the cat that got the cream where he was laying on
His back being stroked by his master Pat.
And that's the story of the invisible cat.
What's that? You think, the story of the invisible cat was a load
Of old tat and you want your money back..........................
Look there's no need to get catty now!
Still I suppose I can hardly blame you for that,
After all that's two minutes of your life
You're never going to get back!

BeWaRe Of tHe VaCuUm CLeAnEr
(It SuCkS)

Beware of the vacuum cleaner.
It's meaner than a grizzly bear as it hoovers
Spiders, flies, and dust mites up off the cellar stairs.

Beware of the vacuum cleaner.
It really hates to share.
It sucks up everything in site,
Because it really doesn't care.

Beware of the vacuum cleaner.
It's meaner than a dinosaur.
When it roars and opens its big wide jaws.
Here it comes. It's time to run
As it sweeps along the floor.

Beware of the vacuum cleaner
Especially if it hasn't been fed.
Yes, if you're playing hide and seek
I wouldn't hide under the bed.

Beware of the vacuum cleaner.
If I were you I'd hide.
Because you never know when its mouth is open
And you'll end up inside.

Beware of the vacuum cleaner
Because it really, really sucks,
And if you get in its way
You might just be out of luck!!

YoU'Re GoOsE HaS BeEn CoOkEd

I own a flock of geese
That won't leave me in peace,
And if they don't soon cease that racket
Then they'll end up deceased in a frozen packet!

OnCe UpOn A RhYmE

Once upon a rhyme
A long, long time ago
So long ago in fact
I can't remember how the rest of the story goes!

My SaT NaV iS A BiT Of A ChAv.

My Sat Nav is a bit of a Chav.
It says to me for a laugh, 'Why don't you rev up the engine
mate
And turn the incar stereo up full blast?'

My Sat Nav is a bit of a Chav.
And its first words to me when I get in the car are,
'Was I talking to you though, was I though, was I talking to
you? but was I though, was I talking to you though?'
And we have to go through that whole rigmarole every time
Before we can go.

My Sat Nav is a bit of a Chav.
When I get in the car its says, 'Lets 'ave it mate and ta
And where's the nearest bar?'
And when we're in a traffic jam it starts to swear
And instead of politely asking to stop to go to the loo
Says rather coarsely 'Gav I need to use the lav.'

My Sat Nav is a bit of a Chav
And when we drive past some good looking girls
It wolf whistles and blows the horn and shouts out loudly
'Why not come in here girls and I'll keep you nice and warm?'

My Sat Nav is a bit of a Chav.
And it doesn't seem to care
And its favourite saying seems to be, 'get in there!'
I can't bear it any longer and it's driving me to despair.
Still to be fair while I've got my Sat Nav in my car
I know nobody will steal it they just wouldn't dare!

WhAt'S tHe ScOrE ?

East Fife   4   Forfar   5

That was the so called famous score
But do you want to know what the actual score was?
Well, it was a boring O-O draw!

Football note: This rhyme was based on a now legendary
                Score between East Fife and Forfar Athletic
                That was supposed to have appeared on a
                Vidie printer on a football results show called
                Final Score.
                But it never actually happened, or did it?
                Forget the Loch Ness monster mystery or
                Big foot or U.F.O.s because it's this mystery
                That seems to grow a little bigger every year
                A bit like Pinochio's nose!

ThReE ChEeRs FoR TrEeS

Three cheers for trees,
That's something I strongly believe,
Because without them we just couldn't breathe.
So if you see one in passing
Show them some love give 'em a hug.
Reach up and give one of their branches a high five
And say, 'Thanks for keeping me alive.'

Three cheers for trees you're cool,
And without you (and I don't mean to be rude)
We're screwed!
And like tree huggers. You'd get some funny looks
And people shouting out things like,
'You must be barking mad,'
Or, 'Are you completely out of your tree?'
But trees nullify the carbon monoxide we insist on
Putting into the air we breathe, which is cool
And shows tree huggers are not such fools after all.

Three cheers for trees,
And dogs love trees because up against them
They frequently pee
Which for them is a big relief.
Conkers come from trees but we don't let our kids
Play conkers at school these days,
Which to me is completely bonkers but typically P.C.!

Continued over the page:

And leaves love trees and trees love leaves
Because they're like their children and they've both
Become quite attached to each other until one day a strong
Wind comes along and then they both go their separate ways,
Looking for some answers that are blowing in the wind.

Three cheers for trees,
Birds love trees because there they build their nests
Especially magpies who use the leaves to cover up
The shiny objects they regularly thieve.
Cats, hats, kites and footballs all love trees
Because without them they'd have nothing to get stuck in
Or at least that's the way it seems to me!

And they say if a tree falls in a forest
And there's no one around to see it fall
It makes no sound which is quite profound.
But I bet a penny to a pound is complete nonsense……..
Unless of course it lands on a very, very large eiderdown!

Three cheers for trees,
For without them Newton would have never have discovered
Gravity, yes I know that's a bit of a stretch,
But it'll do for me.
And I don't want to preach but don't cut down the air that we
Breathe and if you do replant a tree,
It'll make you feel good just you wait and see,
Because trees we really need

Yes, THREE CHEERS FOR TREES!!

HoW AniMaLs ReAcT tO BeiNg InSuLtEd

A rat would simply say 'Shut your trap
Or I'll shut it for you.'
A bandicoot would just scoot in case you decided to shoot.
A centipede would just leg it.
A komodo dragon would get all fired up and probably
Spontaneously combust.
A snake would say 'bite me.'
A boa constrictor would let out a strangulated cry
And then you'd die.
A chuckawalla would throw something heavy at you.
A skunk would yell you smell or you stink, which let's face
It isn't much of a comeback and a bit like the pot calling
The kettle black.
A panda would give you a black eye or two.
A fighting fish need I say more?
A wombat certainly wouldn't be afraid of a bit of arm
To arm combat.
A zebra would be very cross in fact I wouldn't advise
Crossing a zebra (well not without looking first, that is!).
Most birds would fly off the handle, apart from a toucan
Which would just repeat the insult back to you line for line
Or parrot fashion if you like.
A mocking bird (I wouldn't insult your intelligence!).
Cattle would be driven to drink I think.
A worm would turn on you.
A frog would tell you to hop it
(I bet you didn't see that last one coming!)

Continued over the page:

A toad would probably goad you into throwing a few more
insults his way before hopping across the road after reading
The green cross code.
A cat would get into a flap before needing a long nap.
A bee would deliver a stinging rebuke.
A wasp would tell you to buzz off.
A crocodile wouldn't come to any snap decisions it would
Smile and then swallow you whole.
An electric eel would be so shocked by your behaviour it
would be lost for words.
A great white shark would just bite your head off.
A gnu would just tell you to SHOO! but I've told you before
you must never let a gnu tell you what to do!!
A grizzly bear would swear at you before tearing you limb
From limb (though why anybody would want to insult a
Grizzly bear, I can only think they must have a death wish!)
A koala bear would stare wildly at you before falling out of his
tree drunk on eucalyptus leaves.
A kangaroo would jump down your throat.
A turtle would go into its shell.
A great dane would give you dogs abuse.
A monkey would swing for you.
A mouse would just go quiet.
A donkey would call you a silly ass!
A lion would roar and then give you what for.
A giraffe would laugh in your face (but only if you were up
A ladder at the time)
A pig would retort with a dismissive snort.
In short be very careful before you get into any altercation
whatsoever with a creature from the animal kingdom,
If you know what's good for you that is!

MONSTERS

HAIRY,
SCARY,
LET'S BEWAREY.
BITING,
FRIGHTENING,
AS FAST AS LIGHTNING.
COWERING,
SCOWLING,
ALWAYS HOWLING.
MOANING,
GROANING,
ROAMING,
MOUTH FOAMING

MONSTERS!

The QuEsTiOn MaRk ?

In a written quiz
The question mark
Is waiting at the end of every line
Like a coiled snake ready to strike
If you don't get the answer right!

EiNsTeiN A Go-Go

Einstein was cool
And the greatest mind of them all,
In a universe that's very big
From a planet that's very small.
With his grey frizzy hair
And his $E=MC2$
Einstein was like a great big old cuddly bear!

GhOsT BuSt Up

'You're dead to me,' said the ghost to the
ghoul
Storming off through the nearest available wall
The ghoul replied in a disembodied voice
Just as the ghost was disappearing from view
'You're not all there chum.' before he coolly
Turned and floated off down the hall!

Knock, knock who's there?
No-body the ghosts that were knocking
Have all disappeared into thin air!
After eating a meal Why do ghosts still feel
empty inside? Because all they ever eat is
Air pie! after this joke I expect a deathly hush!

NOt A ShOrT LiSt

This is a list of my favourite lists.
A list of girls I'd like to kiss.
A list of things I'd never miss,
(Like going to the dentists or watching *the Apprentice*).
A list of my favourite potato chips.
A list of actors who've played Oliver Twist.
A radio play list. (Which should include Brahms & Liszt)
A shopping list (With all my favourite foods on
like potato chips and spicy dips).
A list of all the things I want to do before I die.
(Including swimming with sharks and doing a sky dive).
A list of my favourite groups. (Inc. The XX & Cherry Ghost)
A list of my favourite soups. (Including the Primordial soup!)
As you can see this is a long list not a short list!
A list of magic spells.
A list of things to do in bed when I'm feeling unwell.
A list of things that give you a lift.
(like a balloon ride or receiving a gift).
A list of things that make you miffed.
(Like getting stuck in a lift or receiving a recycled gift).
A list of my favourite games. (Kiss chase & hopscotch!)
A list of pantomime dames! (You've got to be kidding me!)
(Only because it rhymes with games!).
Right I just need to do a quick check list to make sure I haven't
Missed any list off my list of lists,
Especially as I'm feeling a little listless!
Then I'm going off to sleep to dream of all the girls
I'd like to kiss!

TeN ThiNgS 2 Do B4 U DiE

1. Be born (a good place to start)

2. Sail around the Matterhorn.

3. Stroke a sabre toothed tiger.

4. Climb the Eiger.

5. Swim with a great white shark.

6. Visit a safari park (you can kill two birds with one stone by stroking the tiger while you're there if you dare!)

7. Ride on a camel.

8. Swim the Channel.

9. Sky dive (Providing you've survived the other seven things to do before you die on your list)

1O. Say goodbye!!

Although if you're a little less adventurous instead of doing all
The things on this list you could go down the pub and get......
.........involved in a nice quiet game of dominoes or whist and
Order an orange juice and a bag of salt & vinegar crisps!

HiGhFaLuTiN NeWtOn FrOm LuToN

There was a young man called Newton
Who with words could be highfalutin
He'd babble away all night and all day
Which according to Newton his Dr. put down to a hi-metabolic
rate too many carbohydrates, isotonic re-hydrating sports
drinks and gluten!

What Newton's Dr from Luton actually said putting the boot in
Was for putting two words in where one would do
Newton needed shootin'!

Footnote: Highfalutin means pompous

ThE StOrY Of WaNdA tHe WoNdErFuLlY WiCkEd WiTch
& WaLtEr tHe WeAsLeY WiCkEd WiZeNeD WiZaRd

ONE DAY ON A SUNDAY, WALTER THE WEASLEY WICKED WIZENED WIZARD WAS AWOKEN BY THE DAWN CHORUS, TWO COCKERELS, FOUR LARKS AND THREE CUCKOOS. 'OH HOW I HATE BEING AWOKEN BY THE DAWN CHORUS,' HE SAID, 'THEY'RE ALL DRIVING ME CUCKOO WITH THEIR AWFUL BALLYHOO EVERY MORNING, SIX THIRTY RIGHT ON CUE. OH HOW I WISH THEY'D ALL GET BIRD FLU.
THIS MORNING ALL I WANTED TO DO WAS LIE IN BED,' HE SAID.
'I WOULDN'T MIND SO MUCH IF THEY COULD ACTUALLY SING BUT NONE OF THEM CAN HOLD A TUNE, TO ME IT ALL SOUNDS LIKE A DIN.'
SO WALTER, NOT BEING IN A PARTICULARLY GOOD MOOD, A PARTICULARLY BAD MOOD, YES BUT HARDLY EVER A PARTICULARLY GOOD MOOD, CLIMBED OUT OF BED, PICKED UP HIS MAGIC WAND AND IN ONE FOWL SWOOP TURNED THE DAWN CHORUS, TWO COCKERELS, FOUR LARKS AND THREE CUCKOOS INTO A RATHER TASTY CHICKEN STEW. 'OH YES,' SAID WALTER WITH A SMILE, A MILE WIDE 'CHICKEN STEW, YES THAT'LL DO NICELY FOR MY BREAKFAST. I WAS GETTING FED UP WITH THOSE FLAKES OF CORN EVERY MORN.' (OBVIOUSLY IT WASN'T A SMILE A MILE WIDE. 'SHODDY WRITING,' SAID THE AUTHOR, MORE THAN A LITTLE SURPRISED TO BE INCLUDED IN HIS OWN STORYLINE. 'THAT'S ONE THING I JUST CAN'T ABIDE,' CHIDING HIMSELF NOT BEING ABLE TO HIDE HIS OWN DISPLEASURE WITH THE LINE 'A SMILE A MILE WIDE.')

192

AFTER WALTER THE WEASLEY WICKED WIZENED WIZARD HAD FINISHED
THE CHICKEN STEW, HE WASN'T SURE WHAT NEXT TO DO. MMMM, HE
THOUGHT, WHAT TO DO, WHAT TO DO....... 'I KNOW I'LL GO INTO THE
WAILING WOODS AND TURN A TREE INTO A BAT OF SOMETHING EQUALLY
WICKED LIKE THAT. YES WHAT A WIZARD OF A WHEEZE THAT WOULD
BE,' SAID WALTER FEELING EXTREMELY PLEASED WITH HIMSELF.
WALTER, FORGETTING IT WAS CALLED THE WAILING WOODS FOR A GOOD
REASON WHICH WILL SOON BECOME EVIDENT TO WALTER AND TO YOU
TOO.
TO BE HONEST, WALTER WASN'T THAT GREAT AT BEING WICKED, BUT HE
FELT LIKE ALL THE POSITIONS FOR THE GOOD WIZARDS WERE TAKEN,
LIKE MERLIN AND HARRY POTTER. HE WAS TRYING TO MODEL HIMSELF
ON THE WIZARD OF OZ BUT SO FAR ON THAT SCORE HE WAS FAILING
PRETTY MISERABLY, THOUGH TURNING THE DAWN CHORUS INTO A
CHICKEN STEW WAS DEFINITELY A STEP UP IN THE WICKEDNESS STAKES,
AS FAR AS WALTER WAS CONCERNED. 'RIGHT LET'S GO, TIME WAITS FOR
NO WIZARD,' HE SAID OUT LOUD TO THE ANTIQUE DESK WHICH WALTER
HAD TURNED FROM AN INANIMATE OBJECT TO AN ANIMATE OBJECT, SO
THE DESK WOULD OPEN ITS DRAWS FOR HIM ON COMMAND. WELL, IT
SAVED ON ALL THAT FIDDLE FADDLING ABOUT WITH DRAWS THAT WERE
ALWAYS GETTING JAMMED.
'THAT'S THE TROUBLE WITH ANTIQUE DESKS THEY'RE JUST TOO OLD.'
WALTER WOULD SAY 'STILL THEY'RE WORTH A FEW QUID SO I'M
CERTAINLY NOT GOING TO GIVE THIS ONE AWAY CHEAPLY ON EBAY.'
THE SPELL WALTER HAD PUT ON THE ANTIQUE DESK WORKED LIKE A
CHARM AND THE DESK COULD OPEN AND SHUT ITS DRAWS ON COMMAND,

REFILL THE INK WELL, DUST AND POLISH ITSELF UP AND IF NEED BE MAKE WALTER A CUP OF TEA. YES THIS DESK NEW ITS PLACE, (IN THE CORNER NEXT TO THE BUDGIE'S CAGE.)

WALTER HAD NOW STEPPED OUTSIDE, IT WAS A COLD GREY MISERABLE MORNING THE SORT OF MORNING A WEASLEY WICKED WIZENED WIZARD LIKE WALTER COULD ONLY HAVE WISHED FOR (AS IT HAPPENED HE DID WISH FOR IT!), WALTER SET OFF TO THE WAILING WOODS AT A BRISK PACE EXCITED BY THE PROSPECT OF TURNING SOME POOR UNSUSPECTING TREE INTO A BAT. HE ALSO HOPED THAT IN THE TREE WOULD BE A CAT.

WHAT A SHOCK THE CAT WOULD GET, WALTER THOUGHT WHEN I TURN THE TREE INTO A BAT. THOUGH THE TREE MIGHT WELL ENJOY BEING TURNED INTO A BAT HAVING BEEN ROOTED TO THE SPOT FOR SO MANY YEARS.

FIVE MINUTES LATER WALTER HAD REACHED THE WAILING WOODS HAVING GOT FED UP WITH WALKING SO HE DID A QUICK WALKING SPELL AND IT GOT HIM TO THE WOODS IN FIVE SECONDS FLAT. 'WOW!' WALTER SAID, 'THAT WAS AN INVIGORATING WALK I RECKON BY THIS TIME NEXT YEAR I'LL BE FIT ENOUGH TO RUN A MARATHON.' WALTER LAUGHED TO HIMSELF KNOWING FULL WELL IT WAS ONLY THE MAGIC SPELL THAT HAD GOT HIM TO THE WAILING WOODS IN DOUBLE QUICK TIME.

AS WALTER GOT CLOSER TO THE WAILING WOODS HE REMEMBERED WHY THE WOODS WERE GIVEN THEIR NAME. FOR THE WOODS WERE WAILING FOR ALL THEY WERE WORTH.

'OH SHUT UP,' SAID WALTER 'WHAT HAVE YOU GOT TO WAIL ABOUT? YOU'VE GOT NO WORRIES, IT'S NOT AS IF YOU'RE GOING TO BE CUT

DOWN IN YOUR PRIME LIKE TREES IN THE RAINFOREST, ALL YOU DO IS STAND THERE ALL DAY LONG, YOU WOODS DON'T KNOW YOU'RE BORN YOU HAD BETTER CUT OUT ALL THAT UNNECESSARY HULLABALOO OR I'LL TURN YOU INTO A CHICKEN STEW TOO.

I HALF EXPECT A DIN WHEN I STEP INTO TOWN WITH ALL THOSE CHAVS AROUND DRIVING THEIR SOUPED UP CARS AND PLAYING THAT LOUD FLIP FLOP SOUND, BUT THIS IS A WOOD IT'S SUPPOSE TO BE ALL PEACE AND TRANQUILLITY.
THE WAILING WOODS MUCH TO WALTER'S SURPRISE, NOW SUITABLE CHASTISED STOP WAILING, OR IF IT DIDN'T, WAS NOW ONLY WAILING ON THE INSIDE.
IN THE MIDDLE OF THE WAILING WOODS, WHICH WERE NO LONGER WAILING WAS A WOODEN HUT WHERE TRAVELLERS WOULD SOMETIMES ENTER FOR A BRIEF REST BEFORE THEY CONTINUED ON THEIR WAY. WALTER OPENED THE DOOR OF THE HUT. THE HUT MADE THE OBLIGATORY CREAKING NOISE WHICH IT FELT IT SHOULD DO BEING AN OLD WOODEN HUT IN THE MIDDLE OF A WAILING WOOD IN A MAGICAL STORY. 'OKAY,' SAID WALTER TO THE HUT, 'IT'S ONLY ME, WALTER THE WEASLEY WICKED WIZENED WIZARD, THERE'S NO ONE TO IMPRESS HERE.'
'SORRY,' SAID THE WOODEN HUT, 'OLD HABITS DIE HARD.'
WELL THEY CERTAINLY SEEM TO IN THIS NECK OF THE WOODS WALTER THOUGHT.
WALTER ENTERED THE HUT AND CLOSED THE DOOR BEHIND HIM, MINUS THE CREAKING. AS HE DID HIS EYE CAME UPON A SHELF IN THE CORNER

195

OF THE ROOM, SITTING ON THE SHELF WAS AN ELF WEARING A GREAT
BIG FROWN.
'WELL DON'T JUST STARE AT ME. GET ME DOWN, GET ME DOWN,' THE
ELF SAID, GIVING WALTER A BIT OF A DRESSING DOWN.

'WHAT ARE YOU DOING UP ON THAT SHELF'?' SAID WALTER TO THE ELF.
'I'M NOT AN ELF,' SAID THE ELF, SOUNDING A LITTLE UPTIGHT BECAUSE
SHE HAD BEEN LEFT ON THE SHELF. 'I'M, A WITCH AND MY NAME IS
WANDA,WANDA THE WONDERFULLY WICKED WITCH.'
'WELL YOU DON'T LOOK MUCH LIKE A WITCH TO ME.' SAID WALTER,
TRYING VERY HARD TO HIDE A SMILE THAT HAD SLOWLY BEGUN TO
CREEP ACROSS HIS WIZENED FEATURES.
'WELL YOU CAN TAKE IT FROM ME, I AM A WITCH,' SAID THE WITCH WHO
WAS GETTING MORE AND MORE EXASPERATED WITH WALTER.
'I AM A WITCH, I AM,' THE WITCH SAID REPEATING HERSELF WHILE
STILL MANAGING TO LOOK REMARKABLY LIKE AN ELF. 'WELL IF YOU
ARE WHAT YOU SAY YOU ARE,' SAID WALTER, 'HOW ON EARTH DID YOU
GET STUCK ON THIS HERE SHELF.?'THE ELF WITCH, WITCH ELF, NOW
EVEN I DON'T KNOW WHICH IS WHICH, SAID THE AUTHOR LOOKING A
LITTLE BEMUSED BY THE TWISTS AND TURNS IN HIS OWN STORY.
'A WICKED WIZARD TURNED ME INTO AN ELF AND LEFT ME HERE ON
THIS SHELF ALL BY MYSELF,' SAID THE WITCH.
'I'M A WICKED WIZARD,' SAID WALTER, 'IT WASN'T ME WAS IT, I'VE GOT
SUCH A TERRIBLE MEMORY I'M ALWAYS TURNING THINGS INTO OTHER
THINGS AND FORGETTING TO TURN THEM BACK?'

'OH NO IT WASN'T YOU,' SAID WANDA, 'THIS WICKED WIZARD WAS FAR
BETTER LOOKING, NO DISRESPECT INTENDED.' BUT IN TRUTH WALTER
WAS OFFENDED UNTIL HE REMEMBERED A LONG TIME AGO
HE'D PUT A SPELL ON HIS BATHROOM MIRROR SO HE WOULD ALWAYS
LOOK TWENTY YEARS YOUNGER.

MOST OF THE TIME HE ONLY REMEMBERED THIS WHEN HE CAUGHT HIS
OWN REFLECTION IN THE STREAM AT THE BACK OF HIS HOUSE AND
WHENEVER HE DID HE'D LET OUT A LOUD BLOOD CURDLING SCREAM
AND THEN SAID, 'IS THAT REALLY ME?' THEN HE'D GO 'OH YES, I
REMEMBER, I'M A WEASLEY WICKED WIZENED OLD WIZARD, ANYWAY
THAT'S WHAT PROPER WIZARDS ARE SUPPOSE TO LOOK LIKE, NOT LIKE
THESE NEW AGE WIZARDS LIKE HARRY POTTER, THEY'RE SO YOUNG
THEY HAVEN'T EVEN STARTED TO SHAVE. I WOULDN'T MIND IF THEY
OCCASIONALLY MISBEHAVED BUT THEY'RE ALL SO HOLIER THAN THOU.
WOULDN'T IT BE GREAT IF HARRY POTTER TURNED OUT TO BE A BIT OF
A ROTTER AND THREW ALL NIGHT PARTIES, THEN I'D HAVE A LITTLE
MORE DISRESPECT FOR HIM?'
'SO, THIS WIZARD,' SAID WALTER, 'ANYBODY I MIGHT KNOW?'
'I DOUBT IT,' SAID WANDA. 'THIS WIZARD WANDERED IN FROM SOME
OTHER MAGICAL FANTASY OR OTHER. THERE ARE SO MANY AROUND
THESE DAYS IT'S HARD TO KEEP UP WITH THEM ALL. NOW GET ME
DOWN, I'M FED UP WITH BEING AN ELF.'
'OKAY, DON'T GET YOUR KNICKERS IN A TWIST I DON'T HAVE A MAGIC
WAND YOU KNOW, WELL ACTUALLY I DO I SUPPOSE I COULD TRY A SPELL
OR TWO, I'M SURE WE'LL GET YOU DOWN, IN TWO SHAKES OF A

UNICORN'S TAIL.' HALF A DOZEN SHAKES OF A UNICORNS TAIL LATER
WALTER STILL HADN'T GOT WANDA DOWN.
WANDA WAS NOW BACK TO HOPPING UP AND DOWN, THE FROWN NOW BACK
ON HER ELFIN LIKE FEATURES. 'GET ME DOWN, GET ME DOWN,' CRIED
WANDA, SOUNDING VERY FED UP. 'I'M TIRED OF ALL THIS HANGING
AROUND.'
'LOOK GIVE IT A REST,' SAID WALTER, 'I'M DOING MY BEST.'
'WELL YOUR BEST IS CLEARLY NOT GOOD ENOUGH,' SAID WANDA HAVING
A LITTLE BITCH.

'LOOK STOP SHIRKING AND GET THIS SPELL WORKING,' SAID WANDA
PUTTING HER HEAD IN HER HANDS, 'BECAUSE IF YOU DON'T, WHEN I DO
EVENTUALLY GET DOWN FROM THIS SHELF, YOU'RE DEAD!'
BUT TRY AS HE MIGHT, LONG DAY FOLLOWED LONG NIGHT, WITH NO END
IN SIGHT, POOR OLD WALTER JUST COULDN'T GET THE SPELL RIGHT.
'NEVER FEAR,' WALTER CRIED, 'THE ONLY FEAR IS OF FEAR ITS-ELF.'
WANDA WAS NOW WILDLY STARING DAGGERS IN WALTERS DIRECTION 'I'M
IN NO MOOD FOR JOKES,' WANDA SAID SLIGHTLY GOING OFF HER HEAD.
'LOOK,' SAID WALTER, 'IT'S ONLY A MATTER OF TIME BEFORE I GET THE
RIGHT MAGICAL RHYME. LET'S SEE,' WALTER STARED INTO THE
DISTANCE, MMMM, 'WHAT ABOUT THIS ONE.?'
'HOCUS POCUS A SWARM OF LOCUSTS,' BUT BEFORE WALTER COULD
FINISH THE SPELL, WANDA JUMPED IN. 'NO, NO, SHE CRIED I HAVE NO
DESIRE TO BE TURNED INTO A SWARM OF LOCUSTS ANYMORE THAN I
WANTED TO BE TURNED INTO AN ELF STUCK ON THIS UNCOMFORTABLE
HARD WOODEN SHELF.'
'CHILL-AX,' SAID WALTER, 'OR YOU'LL SPONTANEOUSLY COMBUST.......'

THEN ALL OF A SUDDEN, AS IF BY MAGIC, A WITCH CAME THROUGH THE DOOR OF THE WOODEN HUT AND ON SEEING WANDA'S PREDICAMENT SAID TO WANDA, 'DON'T CRY, LET ME TRY.' THE WITCH TOOK OUT HER WAND WAVED IT SEVERAL TIMES IN WANDA'S DIRECTION AND CHANTED THE FOLLOWING WORDS, 'HITCH SNITCH WITHOUT A GLITCH TURN THIS LITTLE TITCH BACK INTO A WITCH,' AND ALTHOUGH WANDA WASN'T THRILLED ABOUT BEING CALLED A LITTLE TITCH, IT DID SEEM TO DO THE TRICK BECAUSE A FEW SECONDS LATER AND WITH THE OBLIGATORY PUFF OF SMOKE WANDA WAS NOW STANDING ON THE FLOOR, EVERY INCH THE WICKED WITCH SHE WAS BEFORE, WARTS AND ALL.

WANDA WAS SO PLEASED AND EXTREMELY RELIEVED SHE WAS NO LONGER AN ELF, LEPT UP AND DOWN THE FROWN NOW GONE, REPLACED BY A BIG TOOTHY GAPY SMILE. WHEN WANDA HAD CALMED DOWN SHE THANKED THE WITCH AND APOLOGISED TO WALTER FOR BEING A LITTLE TETCHY AND A BIT OF AN OLD GRUMPS BAG. 'WHERE DID YOU SPRING FROM?' WANDA SAID TO THE WITCH.
'WELL,' SAID THE WITCH, 'I HEARD ON THE MAGICAL GRAPEVINE THAT A WITCH WAS STUCK ON A SHELF IN THE WOODEN HUT AND A WEASLEY WICKED WIZENED WIZARD CALLED WALTER WASN'T HAVING MUCH LUCK TURNING HER BACK INTO A WITCH FROM AN ELF.
'SO I THOUGHT I'D COME ALONG AND SEE IF I COULD HELP.'
'WELL LUCKY YOU DID,' SAID WANDA, 'OTHERWISE I'D STILL BE AN ELF STUCK ON THE SHELF TILL DOOMSDAY.'
'NO PROBLEM,' SAID THE WITCH, 'BY THE WAY WHAT'S YOUR NAME?'
'OH I DON'T HAVE A NAME,' SAID THE WITCH, 'I JUST GO BY THE TITLE OF THE WHITE WITCH.'

'YOU MEAN THE WHITE WITCH FROM THE LAND OF NARNIA IN THE LION THE WITCH AND THE WARDROBE?

'YES, THAT'S RIGHT,' SAID THE WHITE WITCH, SOUNDING PLEASED THAT SOMEBODY HAD ACTUALLY HEARD OF HER. 'YOU'RE REALLY FAMOUS,' SAID WALTER A LITTLE BEWITCHED BY THE WHITE WITCH AND THEN LENT OVER AND GAVE HER A KISS. THE WHITE WITCH WENT BRIGHT RED. 'OH,' SHE SAID, 'IT'S BEEN A LONG TIME SINCE I'VE BEEN KISSED, THAT'S SOMETHING I'VE REALLY MISSED. YOU SEE IN THE LAND OF NARNIA I'M A BIT OF A TYRANT AND EVERYBODY'S SCARED OF ME.'

'ME TOO,' SAID WANDA

'ME THREE,' SAID WALTER. WANDA AND THE WHITE WITCH LOOKED AT WALTER AND BURST OUT LAUGHING. 'OKAY,' SAID WALTER, 'SO THEY'RE NOT SCARED OF ME, BUT THEY'RE A LITTLE NERVOUS WHEN THEY SEE ME COMING DOWN THE STREET.'

AS FAR AS WANDA AND THE WHITE WITCH WERE CONCERNED WALTER THE WEASLEY WICKED WIZENED WIZARD WAS A BIT OF A WISHY-WASHY WIZARD IN THE WORLD OF WITCHCRAFT AND WIZARDRY.

THEN ALL THREE, WALTER, WANDA AND THE WHITE WITCH ALL WENT HOME FOR SOME CUCUMBER SAND-WITCHES AND A NICE CUP OF EARL GREY TEA. ACTUALLY THEY DIDN'T, THEY ALL WENT DOWN THE WAND AND CAULDRON AND GOT MERRY ON REAL ALE.

'GOOD HEALTH TO YOU ALL,' SAID WANDA, GLAD SHE WAS NO LONGER AN ELF THAT WAS ON THE SHELF. A FEW HOURS LATER AND MORE THAN A FEW ALES LATER, THE THREE GOT INTO A BREW HA HA WITH A GROUP OF YOUNG CHAVY WITCHES AND WIZARDS THEN FELL DOWN AN OLD DISUSED WISHING WELL AND WERE NEVER HEARD OF EVER AGAIN.

ACTUALLY THAT'S NOT TRUE EITHER, THEY COULD BE HEARD FOR MILES AROUND FOR WEEKS TO COME YELLING AND CREATING MERRY HELL UNTIL A PASSING WIZARD CALLED HARRY STUMBLED ACROSS THEIR PLAINTIVE CRIES AND EXPELLED THEM FROM THE WISHING WELL.

'OH WELL,' HARRY COULD BE OVER HEARD SAYING, 'ALL'S WELL THAT ENDS WELL.' JUST BEFORE HE BID EVERYONE GOOD DAY AND THEN MAGICALLY DISAPPEARED, REAPPEARING IN ANOTHER MORE LUCRATIVE STORY ABOUT WIZARDS AND WITCHES WHERE HE HAD THE STARING ROLE, WHERE AS IN THIS ONE HE WAS ONLY A BIT PART PLAYER. STILL THE AUTHOR IS VERY GRATEFUL TO MR POTTER FOR TAKING THE TIME OUT IN HIS BUSY SCHEDULE TO APPEAR IN THIS STORY.

'I DON'T CARE WHAT ANYBODY SAYS,' SAID THE AUTHOR 'HARRY'S A GOOD KID AND THAT IS THE STORY OF WANDA THE WONDERFULLY WICKED WITCH AND WALTER THE WEASELY WICKED WIZENED WIZARD.'

OOOH WHAT ON EARTH IS THAT AWFUL SMELL? THE SHOWER'S THAT WAY! WHAT WAS THAT? OH YOU'RE JUST ABOUT TO PERFORM A SMELL SPELL, WELL YOU'D BETTER GET ON WITH IT THEN, MY READERS DON'T WANT TO HAVE TO PUT UP WITH THAT PONG FOR MUCH LONGER, 'I SHOULDN'T HAVE TO SPELL IT OUT TO YOU,' THE AUTHOR SAID TO WALTER, WANDA AND THE WHITE WITCH, TAKING HIS LIFE IN HIS HANDS, AS WALTER, WANDA AND THE WHITE WITCH WERE ALL IN POSSESSION OF SOME SERIOUS MAGICAL FIRE POWER AND IF UPSET COULD TURN YOU INTO A TOAD OR WARTHOG OR A RAT AT THE DROP OF A RATHER POINTY WIZARD'S HAT AND THEN THAT REALLY WOULD BE THAT!

AFTER ALL I WAS GOOD ENOUGH TO RECANT YOUR TALE SUCH AS IT
WAS, THE VERY LEAST YOU CAN DO IS STOP SMELLING THE JOINT OUT.
AAAHHH THAT'S BETTER, THAT SMELL SPELL REALLY WORKS A TREAT,
HAVE YOU THOUGHT OF PATENTING IT. OH YOU'RE NOT PERSONALLY
ALOUD TO GAIN FROM MAGIC, THAT'S A SHAME. WHAT BRIGHT SPARK
THOUGHT THAT ONE UP! MORE POLITICAL CORRECTNESS I PRESUME,
SAID THE AUTHOR, IN A BOOMING VOICE AS HE STORMED OUT OF THE
ROOM!!

LEAVING WALTER APOLOGISING ONE MORE TIME TO WANDA FOR NOT
BEING ABLE TO GET HER OFF THE SHELF. 'I'M SORRY.' HE SAID, 'IT
SEEMS AT THE MOMENT I'M JUST GOING THROUGH A BAD SPELL AS FAR
AS MAGIC'S CONCERNED.' BUT WANDA WASN'T LISTENING SHE WAS TO
BUSY ON HER BLOG RECANTING HER TALE AND READING HER LATEST
EMAILS.

AT THIS POINT THE AUTHOR CAME BACK INTO THE ROOM HIS EYES
LIT UP LIKE A XMAS TREE AND WITH A SMILE A MILE WIDE STRETCHED
RIGHT ACROSS HIS TANNED RUGGED GOOD LOOKING FEATURES,
SAID 'I'VE GOT IT! FORGET WIZARDS AND WITCHES THEY'RE OLD HAT
VAMPIRES ARE WHERE ITS AT!!' THE END.

WhAt'S MoRe ScArY?

What's more scary, a spider or a Hadron Collider?
What's more scary, a swarm of killer bees
Or meeting the real E.T.?
What's more scary, a clown
Or seeing your grandad in a hospital gown?
What's more scary, a vampire
Or walking on a high wire?
What's more scary, a roller coaster ride
Or Dr Jekyll and Mr Hyde?
What's more scary, heights
Or seeing your gran in her lycra pink tights?
What's more scary, a parachute jump
Or a camel with the hump?
What's more scary, Shrek or a Dalek?
What's more scary, the film *SCREAM*
Or a bad dream?
Right you get the gist now do your own list.

WhY BuYiNg An ALbaTrOsS FoR
A PeT MiGht WelL Be
SoMeThInG YoU
LiVe tO ReGreT

Why buying an albatross for a pet might well be something
You live to regret.
Look do I really have to spell it out to you?
Do you really want an albatross in your house wouldn't you
Be far happier with a mouse?
No, nothing but an albatross will do, well don't say
I didn't warn you!
Well for one, buying an albatross is going to cost you.
It's no good penny pinching where the albatross is concerned,
After all you don't want any old albatross dross do you?
Yes, you're going to have to fork out a good few quid
And have you got anywhere big enough for it to live.
I'm not being funny but have you ever considered buying
A giant squid!
I mean let's face it, you're going to need a cage the size of a
jail cell if you're going to pacify the R.S.P.C.A. or the
R.S.P.C.B. if you're going to be pernickety and can you
Imagine the size of its bell that with your neighbours is bound
To create merry hell.
And albatross feed doesn't come cheap, in fact the feed alone
Will have you on your knees, financially speaking that is.
In fact it probably eats more than a horse now, do you see
What you've bought.

Continued over the page:

I expect now you're having second thoughts.
(Or you certainly should be!).
And think of the poor neighbours have you heard how loud
An albatross call is, well when you hear it you'll be quite
Appalled and you'll be lucky if your neighbours don't sue!
And another thing what about the size of its wings when you
See them spread out you're bound like your cat to get into
A flap.
And albatross droppings are far from small and have you
Considered how you're going to cope with it flying up and
Down the hall. Oh well it's your call!
Yes you're certainly going to have to show your albatross
Who's the boss oh, and don't forget its dental floss!
And one final thing have you ever seen an albatross when it
Gets upset? I'm telling you owning one is a bit like putting an
Albatross around your neck!
Well I did my best to put you off buying an albatross as a pet
And owning one will cost you in more ways than one.
Still owning one might be kind of fun.
Well at least in the short run!!

TeN ThiNgS E. T. HaTeS

1. Being late for tea.

2. In his diet not getting enough vitamin E.

3. Because he's an alien not being eligible to apply
   For a bank loan.

4. Not being able to phone home.

5. Constantly having to hide

6. Being taken for a (bike) ride.

7. Feeling alienated and that on planet Earth
   For too long he's lingered.

8. Being accused of being light fingered.

9. Being called a big head.

1O. Yes, along with people who burn the toast
    These are the ten things E.T. hates the most!

UnCLe FrEd

One day Auntie Ed(wina) found Uncle Fred dead
In the garden shed.
Auntie Ed couldn't bear to be too far from Uncle Fred,
So she decided to bury Uncle Fred in the flowerbed next to
His beloved garden shed.
Now every spring when the flowers bloom,
Aunty Ed's face glows and she picks the flowers that she feels
Uncle Fred helped to grow through the wind rain and snow
And then takes them to the local flower show.
And when Auntie Ed wins she grins and says,
'That just goes to show there is life after death,
And I bet those judges don't know,
That Uncle Fred helped those flowers to grow.'
Yes, good old Uncle Fred happily resting in his flower bed!

MoNkEyiNg ArOuNd

I can be found out on the town,
Or outside the animal house just monkeying around
With a gnu, here at the zoo, playing happily
On his didgeridoo.
Or having a ball here at the mall
With a toucan or chatty macaw.

Yes, I can be found out on the town,
Or outside the animal house just monkeying around,
With a giraffe just having a laugh,
Or taking a bath with a smelly galah.
Or with a baboon doing a moon
Outside the window of the zoo keeper's car.

Yes, I can be found out on the town
Or outside the animal house just monkeying around.
Mind you it's true
That's what us monkys do tend to do
How about you?

HiGgLeDy-PiGGLeDY HuILaBALoO

Higgledy-piggledy hullabaloo.
This is a spell I created for you.
Try saying it backwards
It still won't do.
Higgledy-piggledy hullabaloo.

Higgledy-piggledy hullabaloo.
A witch's rant
A wizard's brew
A cuckoo barked
A lion flew
Higgledy-piggledy hullabaloo.

Higgledy-piggledy hullabaloo
An angry aardvark
A soppy gnu,
Of what I am saying I haven't a clue.
Yes, higgledy-piggledy hullabaloo!

ThAt's PiRaNhAs

I bought a piranha as a pet
Which pretty soon I did regret.
I put the piranha in the bath,
Which sounds, I know, a little daft.

I really hadn't got a clue.
I obviously hadn't thought it through.
Because I haven't had a bath for weeks,
And as we speak I've begun to reek.

Yes, I think I say this tongue in cheek,
I'm without a paddle and up the creek.
Still, it's not all bleak.
I might not be able to have a bath,
But at least I can still take a leak!

PoEm FoR 2DaY

2	Hot	2	Cold
2	Fast	2	Slow
2	Wrong	2	Right
2	Dark	2	Light
2	Good	2	Bad
2	Happy	2	Sad
2	Thin	2	Fat
2	Bumpy	2	Flat
2	Hip	2	Square
2	Fair	2	Unfair
2	High	2	Low

2Day we're never satisfied which ever way it goes!

ThE FLiGhT Of tHe HuMmiNg BeE

There's no such thing as a humming bee
But if there was it's plain to see
We'd all have honey for our tea at night
Delivered to our table at the speed of light!

MoDeRn(ish) LolLy StIcK JoKe

What would the Spice Girls say to Father Xmas
If they were all sitting on his knee in Santa's grotto?

' We'll tell you what we want what we really, really want!'
(Admittedly it would have to be a Giant's lolly stick!)

PaWs FoR ThOuGhT

Some cats seem deep in thought at times,
Or does nothing enter their tiny little minds?
Apart from looking cool
And playing with balls of wool,
And scratching fleas from out their fur,
While purring on the kitchen floor.
I'm not to sure,
But I definitely think its paws for thought
……………………………….don't you?

MuM'S tHe WoRd

Mum's the word,
I've often heard it said.
Mostly by my dad when he's done something wrong
And doesn't want her to know or create a song
And dance or stink or pong,
Which if you ask me,
Even though I'm only three,
Sounds some what like an oxymoron.
Which coincidentally is what my mum calls Dad
A lot of the time minus the 'oxy' bit!

I LoVe PoEtRy

I love poetry more that cats
I love poetry more than hats
I love poetry more than birds
I love poetry more than words
I love poetry more than words
More than WORDS!
Did you say more than WORDS
Now you're just being absurd!!

(Now you're being absurd, now you're being absurd!
What about the previous two hundred pages?)

InFiNiTy iS A PrEtTy BiG NuMbEr

Go figure what ever number you think of
Infinity is infinitely bigger!

CrEaTuRe DiScOmFoRtS

I hate the nasty biting gnats,
And all the horrid scratchy cats,
I hate the smelly filthy rats
And all the flying flapping bats.
I hate the dogs that bark so loud
And ones that yap and ones that growl,
And cats that howl and cats that prowl
And even cats that go *meow*!
I also hate the birds that sing
And tiny insects with great big wings,
And slugs and bugs and pigs and hares
And spiders I find upon the stairs,
And mice and voles and moles I've found
And creatures that live far underground,
And sharks and crocodiles and snakes.
I hate them all for goodness sake,
And if I never saw one more
I'd die a happy man for sure!

DaD'S In tHe DoG HoUsE AgAiN

Today my dad's been as quiet as a mouse.
When I asked why, my mum said it's
Because he's in the dog house again.
Yes, I thought this morning he looked dog tired.
Apparently last night Dad was like a bull
In a china shop and he dropped my mum's
Favourite porcelain dish – yes my mum
Really let loose and gave my poor old
Dad dog's abuse.
I bet my dad now wished he was standing
On the river bank where everything is as
Quiet as a mouse.
Well, anything's got to be better than being
In the dog house.
Yes, out of my dad Mum said she doesn't
Want to hear another peep
But one thing I still find puzzling,
If dad's still in the dog house tonight
Where's the dog going to sleep?

Anyway I do hope Mum soon lets Dad out of the dog house
because if he's in there too much longer I think he's going to
go barking mad!!

Words Words Words

Words, words, words, words are absurd.
Words can be over heard.
Words are spoken by birds like toucans and macaws
And are written on walls.
Words are used in blurb and in crosswords.
And when drunk can be slurred.
Words used by Wordsworth, and Tom Stoppard
And by Shakespeare the bard.
Words used on postcards.
Words are easy like Ta or hard like *Je ne sais quoi*.
Words used before a question mark
Or barked by a sargeant major to take you to task.
Words to make you laugh Ha, Ha like Pooh bar or Hoop La.
Words in a paragraph or on a graph in the Daily Star
Or daily Telegraph.
Words in scrabble, like Babble or Rabble or Dabble
Swords spoken or gabbled.
Words used in homework.
Words to drive you beserk.
Words spoken by Capt James T. Kirk.
Words to make you smirk or to make you feel a berk.
Words in rhyme, spoken in time.
Words in a rap recited by a rapper in a baseball cap.
Words in the lining of a hat.
Words in your SATS.
Words can drive you bats!

Continued over the page:

Words said words on the World Wide Web
Words spoken words read words that stay in your head.
Words in a text.
Words spoken by a witch in a hex.
Words used in rhyming slang like Posh & Becks!
Words for a dinosaur tyrannosaurus rex.
Words used by Ant & Dec.
Words are simple. Words are complex.
Words on Twitter words to make you titter
Words to say PICK UP THE LITTER!
Words for telling. Words for yelling. Words for spelling
Words in diction. Words in fiction.
Words, words, words, words used in pop.
Words to catch you on the hop.
Words never stop unless they're at the end of a book
Just before the FULL STOP!

A RoCkEt to tHe StArS

If I had a rocket I'd fly up to the moon.
Then onto Mars through the Milky Way
Past all the stars
Traversing my way to the end of the Universe
Getting back in time for tea
But as I haven't I'll just have to stay inside,
And put my hands in my pockets
And run round and round the room
And then get a rocket from my mum,
Who tells me to go outside and play in the sun!

ThE RaPpiN' ZaPpiN' ALiEn KrEw

We're the Rappin' Zappin' Alien Krew and we've come
From outer space to entertain you.
With our fast flowin' lyrical rap we're out of this world in fact,
In our back to front baseball caps and from you we're not
Taking any crap,
And if you don't climb on board we might just snap
And be forced to attack
And if we do then you had better be prepared to get zappped!
Yes, we're the Rapppin' Zappin' Alien Krew,
And we're here to bamboozle you with our alien slang
We're better than Fifty Cent and the Wu-Tang Clan,
Although I think we're more E.T. than Jay Z if you ask me!
Yes, we've literally got rhymes to blow your mind
So hip hop on board with the Krew otherwise you won't
Know what hit you!
We're the Rappin' Zappin` Alien Krew and we're here
To make you jack and sway so don't get in our way
Or we'll have to get the ray guns out to play
Then your only hope will be to get down on your knees
And pray and what's left of you will probably end up
On intergalactic ebay!!

ThE WoRLd WiDe WeB

I'm sorry but I just don't think it's right
That spiders have their own websites!

As BLaCk As InK

The night sky is as black as ink
But not as black as you might think.
In fact it's not black at all,
It's pink!

Footnote: Space isn't black according to scientists
It's a kind of pinky colour!

WhAt'S tHe PoiNt?

What's under a pointy wizard's hat?
A pointy wizard's head!
How does a pointy wizard's head rest
On a pointy wizard's pillow
On a pointy wizard's bed?
Very uncomfortably I would have said!
What do they do with a pointy wizard's head
When a pointy wizard's dead?
Use it as a headstone instead!

Look don't point the finger at me
I know this rhymes pointless
That's why I put it on page 223!

Do KiTtEnS WeAr MiTtEnS ?

Do kittens wear mittens?
Do doves wear gloves?
Do cats wear hats?
Do stoats wear coats?
Do giraffes wear scarves?
Do fox wear socks?
Do dogs wear clogs?
Do bandicoots wear suits?
Do flies wear ties?
Do ants wear pants?
Do koalas wear balaclavas?
Do bulls wear cagoules?
Do wolves wear shawls?
Do hogs with warts wear boxer shorts?
Now i don't want to be a spoil sport
But i can now respectfully report that neither a kitten or a dove
Or a cat or a stoat or a giraffe or a fox or a dog or
A bandicoot or a fly or an ant or a koala or a bull or a wolf
Or a warthog would be seen dead in such awful togs.
Mind you, i did once see a snail in a shell suit and an owl
that had just got out of the bath wearing a towel which
Was a real hoot!

ThiNgS ThAt GiVe YoU A LiFt

Flying a kite
Taking a helicopter flight
A car (ha, ha, ha!)
A Wonder Bra! (Now you've gone too far!)
A great song (perhaps by Lady GaGa)
A movie about King Kong
(King Kong gave Faye Ray a lift, well am I wrong?)
A piggy back ride when you're five
Having your hair dyed when you're eighty five
An escalator
Mr Motivator
Good news
High heeled shoes
A smiling face that's just got rid of that awful metal brace
A good tan
A fireman!
For a werewolf a full moon
For a witch a ride on her broom
Having money in your pocket
For an astronaut a rocket
An incredible view
For a detective finding a clue
A chocolate bun
Anything that's fun
An acrobat
Doing well in your SATS (if you're allowed to do
                                            them that is!)

Continued over the page:

Rock 'n' roll
Scoring a winning goal
Receiving a hand written letter
Getting a lick from your red setter
A balloon ride
On your wedding day seeing your bride
Anything that fills you with pride
A gift
Finishing a long shift
Healing a rift
Yes, these are some of the things that give us a lift.

SeEiNg ReD

Let me mark your card.
If you're a referee that wants to get ahead
My advice to you would be
If a vampire sees RED don't be CROSS be mellow
And show him a YELLOW.
Because if he's not been fed
And you show him a RED,
You're more than likely to end up DEAD!!

I'Ve GOt A BeE iN My BoNnEt

I've got a bee in my bonnet
I've got a flea in my ear
Yes, bugs really bug me
And I wish they'd all just disappear!

FeAr ItS-ELf

They say the only fear
Is of fear itself
Unless of course you're being chased
By a sabre tooth tiger
And you're a pixie or an elf!

ThAt'S A RaP

Riddles and raps,
Tongue twisters and hats,
Birds and bats and baseball caps.
Similes soliloquies metaphors galore,
Gimmicks, limericks that's bitchin' I'm sure.
Sonnets, phonetics and hullabaloos
Of what I am saying I haven't a clue,
Bling rings and all minging things
I just wanna rap, 'coz I can't really sing.
Flees, bees and five and dimes,
It need not have reason as long as it rhymes.
Verbs, words, adverbs and nouns,
It's not how it reads it's how that it sounds.
So just keep it coming `coz I wanna get down
Yes jump up jump up jump up jump around.
Okay that's a rap now I'm off to read what's on
Snoop Dog's blog today okay word up!

My TeAcHeR's A DrAgOn

My teacher's a dragon . She's got great big wings,
Breathes fire and flies off the handle at the slightest thing.
No, I'm not telling fibs. Last week she flew at me so hard
She nearly broke my ribs.
Like I said. She's always flying off the handle, no, she's
Not a witch, she's a dragon. Can't you get that through
Your head? Her classes fill us with dread.
When I wake up in the morning just thinking about her
Makes me want to stay in bed.
I've lost count of how many times she's set the fire alarm off.
No, I'm not telling tales, when she gets angry fire comes out
Of her nostrils then the alarm goes off every time without fail.
It's hard not to get into a flap when she taps you on the
shoulder snorts roars and gives you what for let's face it when
She's like that she's difficult to ignore.
And when she gets hot under the collar I think to myself *it's*
Just a matter of time before one of us kids she swallows.
Yes, it's worse than being in the horror film *Sleepy Hollow*.
Yes, my teacher's a dragon and a real pain the only thing that
Cools her off is standing out in the rain!
Mind you our new maths teacher is a dragon slayer.
So maybe one day he'll do us all a favour and slay her
So in class I can get back to listening to Dragon Slayer
On my new i-pod player!

NeVeR InSuLt A VaMpiRe

If a vampire insults you never say back to him
Any of the following things:

BITE ME

Buffy The Vampire Slayer Rocks

VAMPIRE WEEKEND SUCK

As do Twilight, True blood, The Vampire Diaries
Interview with the Vampire, The Vampires
Assistant
And Dracula.
Unless you're tired of living that is!

My TeAm'S tHe BeSt

My team's the best, they're better than all the rest,
And I'll support them till the day I die,
And even when they lose and, I give them dogs abuse.
Even when they're wrong, they're right in my eyes.
And I'll argue till I'm blue in the face
If anybody said otherwise.

It was a goal!
It wasn't offside!
Refereeeeeee, are you blind have you lost your mind?
The cat runs and hides,
The rose coloured spectacles working in full effect.
My mum just smiles.

My team wins. I'm over the moon,
And I run round and round the room
Punching the air in pure delight.
And when they lose it's all doom and gloom,
And I hide in my room for the longest time.

It's only a game and most sane people would agree,
But not me because I'm a football fan you see.
And I must admit I think it's funny
How kids these day don't support there local team
But the team that wins everything in sight,
Though they've never ever been to see them play before
Which to me doesn't seem quite right!

Continued over the page:

They should try supporting Accrington Stanley.
They need your support believe you me,
And Accrington's club motto is 'the club that wouldn't die',
Which ends this rhyme nicely.
Although I'm biased as they're my team,
And one day I believe Accrington Stanley will win
The Champions League.
Well, in a parallel universe, maybe!

Remember the smaller clubs are the life blood of football
So go along and see your local team from time to time
They really need your financial and vocal support.

NOt So HaPpY TaLk

All that squawking and talking some birds should be seen
And not heard.
I'm talking of parrots, like toucans and macaws off course.
With all that mimicry and back chat I think I'd rather have
A blood sucking bat, than birds who can repeat words
At the drop of a hat, or a vulture pinning me to the floor.
Yes, they should speak when they're spoken to and not before.
With their loud annoying calls and inane chatter
They're giving me earache as my peace and quiet they
constantly shatter, leaving my nerves in tatters.
I can barely hear myself think these noisy birds are literally
Driving me to drink.
I think I'd rather have an armadillo on my pillow
Or a poisonous snake wrapped around my neck
Or have a black widow spider crawling up my leg
Or have a hippopotamus sleeping in my bed,
Than to have to listen to parrots like toucans and macaws
That often make my ears bleed making me see red.
Still, I suppose being a zoo keeper in a bird house in a zoo,
That's what I'm employed to do!
Perhaps I should get a job in a library instead!

PoEtiC LiCeNcE

Inside the poet's mind
Ideas are quite sublime
But when they hit the page
They sometimes misbehave!

CoMiC VeRSe

Comic verse
Can be somewhat perverse
Especially when you can't
Complete the last verse!

A GeOLOgiSt GEtS RoCkEd

A Linebacker gets Blocked
A Rower gets Coxed
A Ship gets Docked
A Blood Hound gets Foxed
A Diamond Ring gets Hocked
A Pair of Knees get Knocked
A Jaw (that belongs to a chatter box) gets Locked
A Mocking bird gets Mocked
A Warlock gets put in the Stocks
(If he's lucky if not his head ends up on the chopping block)
A Child gets the Chicken Pox
An Electric Eel gets Shocked
A Jack is told to get back in his Box
A Clock gets Ticked Off
A Cook in a Chinese restaurant gets Told Off
For not properly cleaning his Wok
A Boxer gets his ears Boxed
And a Geologist at a Music Festival gets Rocked!
(By Queens of the Stone age and the Rolling Stones!!)

SpEeD ReAdiNg

Books are full of pages
And reading 'em takes me ages
Comics are much more fun
Ten minutes flat and then I'm done!

ThAt'S AlL WrOnG

From Japan there was a young man
Who walking backwards just couldn't stand
He said 'I have tried with the aid of a guide
But on my bottom I constantly land!'

CoWs JuSt FaRt AnD EaT GrAsS

Cows just fart and eat grass
Now that to you may well seem harsh
But what else do they do I ask you?
Apart from making silly mooing sounds
And leaving cow pats on the ground
And sitting on their bums
while soaking up the sun
And being a pain blocking up country lanes
And letting off steam if you know what I mean.
Yes it may well seem harsh but cows just fart and eat grass!

I apologise to all vegetarians but the herd of cows
I recently read this rhyme to were over the moon about it
And on the strength of it have asked me to write their
Autobiography. 'Yes, all we do is fart and eat grass
But we're not short of brains after all we always know
When to sit down just before it rains.'
Anyway I'll have you know some of my best friends
Are cows, Ermintrude from *The Magic Roundabout* for one.
I don't know you can't even write a nonsense rhyme about
Cows these days without creating a fuss and hullabaloo!

ThE IdIoTs GuiDe tO FeNdiNg OfF VaMpiReS

DON'T GO TO TRANSYLVANIA YOU IDIOT!

GeT Up AnD Go

I'm up, I'm hyper, I'm psyched
I'm as high as kite
I'm travelling at the speed of light.
I'm a shooting star and a supernova all rolled into one.
I'm shining brighter than the sun.
I'm primed, I'm wound up tighter than a coiled spring.
I feel like I've got wings,
I'm full of beans so stand clear (if you know what I mean!)
I was born ready, I can't wait to begin.
I'm like a firework ready to go off.
I'm like a jumping jack in fact.
I'm like a speeding bullet, shot from a gun.
I'm all fired up I think I'm going to spontaneously combust.
I'm on top of the world,
I'm number one.
I could run and run and run.
I'm as fast as lightning.
I'm super keen
I reign supreme
Well, I will,
When I eventually get out of bed that is!!

WhAt'S A QuArK?

What's a quark?
Well I'll tell you what a quark's not.
A quark's not an animal that went two by two
Into Noah's Ark,
And it's not a piece of modern art either,
That would just be plain daft (like a lot of modern art!)
Neither is it an old root from a tree in Egypt that will
Enable you to see in the dark and if you thought it was,
Then I can tell you you're way off the mark.
A quark is not a rare type of shark, and if you say it is
Then I'll take you to task.
Nor is it a character out of *Shrek* or *Star Trek*.
Oh, it is a character out of *Star Trek* yes but I think you'll find
I said what is a quark not who is Quark?
A quark is not a small Albanian dog with a very loud bark.
Although over that one there may be a slight question mark.
Nor is it a small island off the Island of Sark.
And it has nothing to do with angels that hark!
And it most certainly isn't a bird like a lark.
Yes it is a cheese but it's spelt qvark!
Right now I've told you what a quark isn't
I suppose you'll be wanting to know what a quark is!
Well, for your information, a quark is any group of
Hypothetical components of elementary particles,
An invented word based on 'the three quarks for muster mark'
in James Joyce's novel *Finnegan's Wake*.
What's a quark? Well you would ask,
Now I bet you don't feel so blinkin' smart!

It'S LiKe A ZoO iN HeRe

'It's like a zoo in here,' said the cockatoo to the gnu,
As he flew into a rage inside his cage.
'It will all end in tears,' said the meerkat to the deer,
As he stuck his fingers in his ears.
'I can't hear myself think,' said the mink to the lynx,
While they were both attempting to watch *The Weakest Link*
And both agreed the noise was far worse than a small child
Washing up in the kitchen sink or a riot in the clink and
Quite frankly it was driving both of them to drink.
'I can't collect my own thoughts,' snorted the hippopotamus,
To the rhinoceros who were both extremely over wrought.
'It's just not fair,' said the kangaroo in deep despair as he was
In the middle of washing his hair.
'I don't mind admitting,' said the kangaroo 'my nerves have got
So bad the slightest noise makes me jump.' and the poor old
Camel well he just got the hump! (now there's a surprise!)
Both the panda and the salamander said with candour they'd
Had enough and were off to tropical climes where they were
Going to build a house in a tree called a jacaranda!
The parrots in the bird house decided the only way they were
Going to get any peace was at the local library 'and that's
Where we're going,' they all squawked, 'even if we have to
walk.'
'Yes,' they all said, 'with all this chatter and talk it's worse than
Fifth Avenue in New York.'

Continued over the page:

The giraffe with his head in the clouds, said the noise didn't
Really bother him and suggested to the other animals in the zoo
If they wanted to avoid the noise they should join the
Local gym.
'Yes, there's such a hullabaloo in here,' said the monkey to the
Emu, 'I can't even concentrate on my sudoku and I think I've
Started to go cuckoo.'
'Yes I agree,' said the ostrich, some of these noisy animals
should be ostracized and banned,'
As he stuck his head in the sand.
The moose said 'I think I've got a screw loose and I don't want
To be a killjoy, but all this annoying noise is worse than the
sound of a vuvuzela or a football stadium tannoy.'
'You're right,' said the Ostrich his feathers a little ruffled and
his voice a little muffled too.
Due to the fact his head was still firmly stuck in the ground.
The animals were peeved and extremely aggrieved and all
agreed that it was like a zoo in here,
But what else can you do when you're living in a zoo other

Than create a great big hullabaloo or organise a coup.
But surely you've got to be cuckoo to organise a coup in a
Zoo when it's you that's causing the hullabaloo, haven't you?

The FaTtEsT CAt iN tHe WoRLd

The fattest cat is my tabby cat and it's getting fatter
And that's a fact.
It's the fattest cat in the world I'm sure
It's five stone something and a little bit more.
It never runs or climbs up trees
Or plays amongst the fallen leaves.
It never chases mice no more or brings dead voles
Up to my door.
In fact all it ever does is snore as it lays upon my kitchen floor.
It eats, then sleeps, then eats once more,
Then repeats the above then starts to snore.
And if it eats too much more it won't get out the kitchen door.
The cat flap I've had to make so wide
An elephant could probably squeeze inside,
Mind you I shouldn't really be so unkind
After all my tabby cat is eighty nine!
In cat years that is!!

TeAcHeRs HaVe EyEs iN
ThE BaCk Of ThEiR HeAdS

It has been said that teachers seem to have eyes
In the back of their heads.
And you'll find it hard to catch a teacher on the hop,
Because they've got ears that can hear a pin drop.
And teachers love to burst your bubble, and they seem
To have a remarkable nose for trouble.
Something else teachers seem to have is super X-ray
Vision or how else would they know when I'm at home
I never do my revision, because I'm watching television.
Also teachers must have their own built in lie detector
Machine because they always seem to know when I'm
Trying to pull the wool over their eyes over why I didn't
Do my homework or why I'm not wearing my school tie.
And how come teachers always seem to know what's going
On behind their backs and seem to have a sixth sense when
They turn around and catch me in the middle of eating a
Quick snack or when I'm cheating in my SATS?
Yes, nothing much gets past them and I'm always getting my
fingers burned. You'd think that's one lesson I would
Have learned.
So it can't come as any great surprise teachers have eyes
In the back of their heads.
Especially our head teacher Mr Wise, he's got eyes every-
where or so he says!

ThE ThiNgS PeOpLe ColLeCt

Beer mats,
Stamps,
Antique lamps,
Marvel comics,
Candles,
Blue Peter annuals,
China pigs,
Clocks,
Jack-in-a-box,
Postcards,
Trains,
Model aeroplanes,
Yo-Yos,
Trolls,
Barbie dolls,
Souvenir plates,
Ties,
Old 45s,
Thimbles,
Hats, videos of *Postman Pat*,
Traffic cones,
Mobile phones,
2OO pounds in Monopoly when you pass go!
Kites,
Chopper bikes,
Meteorites.
Yes the things people collect to some are a delight but to others
Just a load of old junk that should be kept well out of sight!

WhAt If tHe MoOn WaS MaDe Of ChEeSe?

What if the moon was made of cheese?
What cheese would it be made of, let's see?
Would it be made of Gorgonzola cheese?
Well, that's blue and yellowy like the moon
(which is supposed to be made of rock)
And smells like an old sock
And when the moon is crescent shape
Would leave a particularly unpleasant after taste.
And I assume, God the Creator, used a cheese grater to
Fill in some of the craters on the moon.
If you were a mouse and the moon was made of cheese
That would be pretty cool. Mind you, if you ate the whole
Of the moon you'd then be extremely full!
Perhaps the moon would be made of red Leicester
No that's more likely to be Mars.
Maybe Wensleydale cheese or Greek feta. No that would
Be just too crumbly and break up to easily. And if that did
Happen I can only assume that astronauts then would no
Longer be able to walk on the moon.
And what if the moon was made of camembert? That would
Be a complete nightmare; it would be far to creamy and soft
With all those astronauts jumping up and down, think of all
The wear and tear. Yes if you were walking on camembert
It just wouldn't bare your weight, so a message to all
Astronauts: if the moon is made of camembert you had all
Better beware.

Continued over the page:

Perhaps it would be a light cheese like Cheshire cheese
If it were that really would be the bee's knees.
Actually I'm not being funny but bees have got nothing
To do with cheese they make honey.
Mind you, it would be funny if they did because boy
Wouldn't the moon be runny it would just slide off into
Space? An if it didn't still astronauts would get their moon
Boots stuck in it and wouldn't be able to leave the moon,
Yes there's no room for honey on the moon. (That's lunacy!)
Look here's a thought, if a spacecraft were to land on the
Moon wouldn't its landing boosters be so hot the spacecraft
Would just go right through the moon and come out the other
Side?
Then the moon would be left with a great big hole in it.
Yes you're right there are more holes in this story than a slice
Of Dutch cheese!
But is this theory any less credible than the websites that
Claim we never actually landed on the moon, that it was all
A massive hoax perpetuated by N.A.S.A. and the American
Government of the day.
Recently I found a piece of the moon for sale on ebay so
I bought it. You guessed it, it was made of cheese!
All be it a hard stale piece of cheese!
But be in no doubt cheese it was.
Well those are the facts only you can decide whether you
Believe the moon is made of cheese or not
Perhaps it's only fair to say when I wrote this piece for *Cheese
And Wine Monthly* there was a full moon, and I had just
polished off a couple of nice bottles of Albanian red before
I retired to bed!!

KiDs

BELLY ACHING,

WINDOW BREAKING,

MUD CAKING,

ILLNESS FAKING,

NERVE GRATING,

NEVER WAITING,

LATE WAKING,

HEAD SHAKING,

RISK TAKING,

TROUBLE MAKING,

WINDBREAKING

FOR GOODNESS-SAKING KIDS!!!

NeVeR CrOsS A ZeBrA

When you're in the wild you should be fine
As long as you follow the correct procedure.

A. Never cross a zebra

B. Never make a boss-eyed lion cross

C. Never cross the River Nile incase there's a crocodile
    Lurking there who thinks he's the boss

You don't have to follow this procedure
But if you don't it will be your loss!

QuEsTiOn AnD AnSwEr

Question: Excuse my grammer but what's
           not the sharpest tool in the box?

Answer: A Hammer!

FaDiNg DrEaMs

One day all my dreams ended in
The washing machine.
You ask me how, well I'll come clean,
I left my winning lottery ticket
In the back pocket of my faded blue jeans!

InJuStiCe

Injustice you make me want to SHOUT
And the only justice in you
Is taking the word IN OUT!

TiMe FLiEs

For a fly time flies.
One minute it's born
The next it dies, why?
Don't ask me,
I'm a flea and it seems quite wrong
But I don't even get to live that long!

DeAd On My FeEt

The werewolf, said to the vampire,
'As it's a full moon I assume you'll be tucked up
Tightly in your tomb.'
The vampire replied, 'Your dead right,
I can't stand the moonlight.'
The vampire then said to the werewolf, rather
Sarcastically, 'I assume, just for a change you'll be
Out in the howling wind and rain seeing red again.'
The werewolf replied, 'That's right
I'm looking forward to going out tonight for a bite
To eat and giving somebody a nasty fright.'
The vampire then said to the werewolf,
'Well you must be barking mad.
I'm glad I'll be tucked up in bed
Having recently been well fed,
'Coz I'm dead on my feet!'

WiZaRdS WiTh WoRdS nOt

Question: Do wizards use a spell check?

Answer: They do if they can't spell properly!

An ExCEpTiOnAlLy LaMe JoKe

What does a knight of the round table listen to on his iPod player? ......Dragon Slayer!

CoMiC EFFeCt

'I'm not being funny,' said the comedian
Sounding more than a little uptight
'But you've been a terrible audience tonight.'
Some comedian in the audience shouted back
With great delight
'You don't have to tell us you're not being funny mate
After all you haven't managed to be funny all night!'

ShArK AtTaCk iN ReVeRsE

Today a man attacked a great white shark.
The great white shark didn't stand a chance.
He didn't see it coming, he got an awful fright,
When the man sunk his teeth in and took a great big bite.

The great white shark complained,
'What on earth is this man's game?
To attack a Great white shark he surely must be insane.'

The man took another bite.
The shark did not survive.
He ate the tail,
He ate the fins,
He ate everything that was inbetween,
He didn't stop till he'd eaten the lot.
He really must have lost the plot.

When asked why the man ate the great white shark,
He delivered this reply.
'I just felt like a quick bite
And the great white came into sight
I'm really not insane.
I haven't lost the plot.
I was simply suffering from hunger pains'
Some people talk such rot!

WiThOuT WaTeR

Without water what would we do?
For a start, we couldn't flush the loo,
And we'd all smell pretty bad too.
In fact let's face it we'd all be screwed!

Without water we'd be in dry dock
And there would be no Scotch on the rocks.
The sales of water closets would go down the pan
And diving in swimming pools
Would definitely be banned!

Without water the Titanic would never have
Left the land.
Children would never have the sea wash away
Their castles in the sand.
In swimming pools in the school holidays
You wouldn't hear a sound
And ships and boats would never run aground.

Without water you wouldn't see anybody wearing
A snorkel or diving mask
Nobody would ever get eaten by a great white shark.
Canoeists and water skiers wouldn't get far
And cliff diving would hurt like hell
And soon be consigned to the past.

Continued over the page:

Without water, fish and chips would simply be chips.
Nobody would slip in the shower and break their hips.
Surfing wouldn't exist
And teenagers in swimming pools wouldn't give life guards
Any lip!

Without water the sales of water beds would sink overnight.
And the Loch Ness Monster would have nowhere to hide.
Swimming pools would be threatened with massive closures
And skinny dipping would just be indecent exposure!

In short have given it much thought (NONE!)
And I don't mean to be lewd but without water
We're ………SCREWED!!

HiDe AnD SeEk

One day in the jungle a tiger and a monkey
Decided to play a game of hide and seek.
The tiger said to the monkey, 'I'll close my eyes
And I promise I won't peek, while you sneak off
And hide.'
The monkey who was obviously pretty dim because
He didn't realise the tiger was making a monkey
Out of him and taking him for a ride.
Unfortunately for the monkey the tiger lied
(Now there's a surprise!)
The monkey with a quizzical look on his face said,
'I've got no idea where I'm going to hide.'
'Well,' said the tiger, 'if you're looking for a place to hide,
Why not hide inside my mouth there it's nice and dry.
There you can disappear and I'll never find you in
A million years.' (Why do you get the feeling this story
Is all going to end in tears?).
So the monkey, being pretty dim, believed him and
Climbed inside the tiger's mouth to hide.
The tiger counted to five and then ate the monkey alive,
And after the tiger and the monkey's game of
Hide and seek (which for the monkey turned out to
Be pretty bleak)
All that was left of the monkey was the monkey's feet!

And the moral of this tale is a simple one.
Never play hide and seek with a tiger,
No matter how much he promises he won't peek
Otherwise he'll definitely make a monkey out of you!

DoN't Do ThAt!

Don't run
Don't stay out in the sun too long
Don't talk to strangers
Don't stick out your tongue
Don't smoke
Don't drink too much coke
Don't make a din
Don't get soaked to the skin
Don't go too far
Don't bring any tadpoles back in a jar
Don't play in the road
Don't bring back any dead toads
Don't miss your tea
Don't stroke any cats with fleas
Don't brawl
Don't fall off any high walls
In fact don't do anything you shouldn't do
That's what mothers say just before you go out to play!

ThE BoY WhO WaS BoReD tO DeAtH

'I'm bored to death.' the boy said lying on his bed
With his hands clasped behind the back of his head.
His dad replied, 'Well Ned, why don't you do something
Useful instead and get off your bed and go and paint the
Garden shed red?'
'Paint the garden shed red,' said Ned, 'I'd rather chew off my
Own leg than paint the garden shed red.'
So he promptly did and poor old Ned bled to death
And now poor old Ned's no longer bored but dead.
So, let that be a lesson to you.
If you're bored don't chew off your own leg like Ned
Do something more constructive instead and go and paint
Your dad's garden shed red.
Well it's got to be better than being dead like Ned!

CrEaTiNg A BiG ImPaCt

It's a fact that when you stand back
A giant crater creates quite a big impact!

On A HyDiNg tO NoThiNg

One day Dr Jekyll fell out with Mr Hyde
On a bike ride.
Somewhere along the south coast
Where they got into a fight over who was pedalling
The most and rode into a lamp post
And now Dr Jekyll and Mr Hyde are both ghosts!

BuRsTiNg tHe WitChEs BuBbLe

Hubble bubble,
Toil and trouble,
The witch is dead
So bring the shovel.

Bubble hubble
Trouble and boil,
Put the witch
Into the soil.

Hubble bubble,
On the double
Fill her in with
Bricks and rubble.

And when that's done
To end your troubles
Get in a bath
That's full of bubbles!

Ex-SPeLLeD

Why is a wizard so good in a spelling bee?

Because he uses an invisible dictionary!

Presumably he casts a magic spell so only he can see
The invisible dictionary.
Well, why ask me?
I don't know. Some people can be so picky.
But if he's caught I'm sure he'd be put on report
Especially if he was attending Hogwarts
And then he'd get ex-spelled I would have thought.
Mind you, if you were a modern wizard these days
You'd be a lot more high tech and probably use a spell check.
And if you were a witch today and you wanted
To put a hex on somebody you'd probably do it by text!

CoMpUtErS

Computers link things together.
Tell us about the weather.
Drive us to drink push us to the brink.
Don't think and are always on the blink.
Computers help us store our songs
Are always right even when they're wrong.
Are full of jargon use CD roms
Are used to carry out cons.
Computers are a turn off and turn on.
Computers I'd like to shoot.
Computers don't give a hoot
Computers don't compute.
And those ones normally end up in a car boot!
Computers are hip. Computers are square.
Computers have us all tearing out our hair.
Computers at home, computers at school,
Computers are cool, Computers rule.
Computers do what we tell them to do.
(If you're lucky!)
Yes, computers link things together
And if they all suddenly stopped we'd all be lost.
So we all need computers whether we like it or not!

It'S RaiNiNg CAtS AnD DoGs

'It's raining cats and dogs'
  One day I heard my mum say.
  'Well, Mum' I said, 'okay
  Then I'll have to put my hard hat on my head
  Before I go out to play!'

DrAgOn'S YoU'Re FiReD!

Look there's no way to sugar coat this
Dragon's in the den you're dire
And as the wizard's apprentice you've guessed it
You're fired!

A GoLdFiSh's TaLe

I'll be bound I bet a penny to a pound
That goldfish of yours spends all day
Swimming around and around and around
And around and around and around and around
And around and around and around and around
And around and around and around and around
And around and around and around and around
And around and around and around and around
And around and around and around and around
And around and around and around and around
And around and around and around and around
And around and around and around and around!

Sorry what was that you just said,
You think your goldfish is dead!
Well there's my penny and you can keep your pound
But I really wish you had told me that your goldfish was dead
The first time around!!

iT's NOt RoCkEt SciEnCe (Or iS It 2)

Who was it that made this famous quotation?

The moon is magnificent desolation

Answer at the foot of the page:

Answer: Buzz Aldrin the second man to walk on the moon.

ThE PrEciPiTaTiOn RePoRt

Tomorrow it would be a good shout
To take an umbrella with you if you go out
Because as it's a bank holiday
There's bound to be a lot of precipitation about!

Weather that's a good shout or not
Only time will tell
My guess is not and it will probably turn out hot!
Mind you if it's a bank holiday then maybe not!!

SqUaRe EyEs

They say if you watch too much TV
You'll get square eyes.
Well if that's true does that also mean
If you've got square eyes
You can no longer roll your eyes from side to side?
Because if it does I wouldn't be the least bit surprised!

It DeFiNiTeLy iS RoCkEt SciEnCe

What are the most famous words spoken of all time
Which when put together with the question
Also rhyme?

Answer at the foot of the page:

Answer: 'That's one small step for a man, and one giant leap
        For mankind.' Said by Neil Armstrong when he
        Became the first man to set foot on the moon in 1969.

I ShOuLdN't TeAsE My LiTtLe SiStEr

I shouldn't tease my little sister.
I know it's just not right
Or sneak up behind her back and give her a nasty fright
Or put a spider in her bed,
Or lock her in the garden shed,
Or knock her hat from off her head,
Or tell her that her pet hamster's dead,
Or put salt in her tea.
Yes I shouldn't tease my little sister my mum tells me
But why ever not after all she is forty three!

An ALiEn SpOrE

A speck of dirt upon my floor,
Perhaps it's a tiny alien spore.
I would sweep it out the door
But I don't want to break any intergalactic laws,
Or start an intergalactic war,
So I'll leave it there just to be sure,
Like I've done a million times before,
With another million alien spores!

Any excuse not to sweep the kitchen floor!

ThAt's IlloGiCal CaPt !

There was a vulcanologist called Spock
Who was constantly blowing his top
To stop he had tried
But the truth was he lied
'Coz when started he just wouldn't stop!

ThAt's loGiCal CaPt!

Never stop a vulcanologist in mid flow
Especially if his name is Spock
For his bound to blow his top!

BiRtHdAy BLuEs

I have a birthday every year, and every year I live in fear,
Of cakes with too many candles, of which I cannot handle.
And party hats and jokes about my age or getting fat
Which drives me bats from teenagers still sitting their SATS.
And getting useless presents like baggy jumpers
From silly twits that never fit and woolly socks.
I'm surprised some wag hasn't sent me a broken down
Grandfather clock.
Still I suppose it's better to have a birthday than not!

A DuSt MiTe MiGhT

A dust mite might get into a fight with another dust mite
Over who's wrong and who's right.
Or a dust mite might just take flight and flee.
Which I'm sure you'd agree would be quite a sight to see.
Mind you if I was a dust mite and I got into a fight
With another dust mite over who's wrong and who's right
I think I might say to the other dust mite, 'BITE ME!'

SLaPsTiCk

Never slap a stick
Or it'll trip you over
When you least expect it!

ThAt'S BeYoNd ThE PaLe

Jack and Jill went up the hill
To fetch a pale of water
Jack fell down and broke his crown
And Jill just howled with laughter!

SpAcEd OuT

The trouble with extraterrestrials is,
They're so spaced out most of the time
It's almost as if they're living on another planet!

ThE MyStErY Of MuRtLe
ThE GiAnT BLuE TuRtLe

Every night Murtle, the giant blue turtle, would hurtle round
The room at breakneck speed, just before she settled down to
Eat her tea. Which was quite a sight to see and for a giant blue
turtle that's not easy, believe you me.
When Murtle, the giant blue turtle, was asked why she hurtled
Around the room at a breakneck speed just before she settled
Down to eat her tea, she became quite aggrieved and more than
A little peeved, feeling it was an impingement on her privacy
And said, 'please leave me be, because I've just eaten my tea
and now all I want to do is be left alone to watch *Mutant Ninja
Turtles* on dvd.'
It certainly was a strange affliction on that everybody agreed
And not normal behaviour for a giant blue turtle and all were
Very keen to find the key to unlock this rather strange mystery.
And by all, I think I should explain, that Murtle shared a house
With a budgie, a chipmunk, a cat and a bee.
Though why I've got no idea. I'm just telling the story. It's
really got nothing to do with me. I'm happy as long as I get my
Writers fee! Now where were we? Oh yes, the mystery well
The budgie in his cage flew into a rage.
The chipmunk chipped in his two penny's worth and told the
Budgie to behave.
The cat said, 'You're all acting bats. Why should any of you
give a rats what Murtle the giant blue turtle does before she sits
down to eat her tea?'

Continued over the page:

The bee disagreed and put a rather large flea into the cat's ear,
Speaking metaphorically.

Murtle tired of all the fuss, said, 'I will keep my secret till the
day I die.' I think she spoke too soon because no sooner had
she uttered those words she stopped breathing and became
deceased. Well she was two hundred and forty three! Still, at
least, Murtle got her wish, to be left in peace even if it was....
.... permanently!

So unfortunately, well never know why Murtle, the giant blue
turtle, used to hurtle around the room at breakneck speed
before she sat down to eat her tea.

But if you ask me, my guess is, she either had O.C.D. or she
was secretly training for a marathon race and was afraid she
couldn't keep up the pace,

And so took to doing short, fast sprints to improve her stamina,
A trick all marathon runners, and some giant blue turtles use as
part of their training schedule. (Called Fartlek sessions!)

Mind you that's just an educated guess.

Perhaps you have a better explanation to solve the mystery of
Murtle, the giant blue turtle, but if you do please keep it to
yourself because I don't want to know!

Right now I'm off to have a spot of tea and then sit down to
watch *Mutant Ninja Turtles* on dvd with my friends the
Budgie, the chipmunk, the cat and the bee and I know this isn't
the first time I've said this but if you believe that you'll believe
anything!!

ThiNgS We LoVe tO HaTe

Bees,
Peas,
Sharks,
The dark,
Dogs that constantly bark,
Slugs,
Bugs,
Dentists,
Most of the contestants on *The Apprentice*,
Snakes,
Marzipan cakes,
Rats,
Hissing cats,
Salads,
8O's power ballads,
Some of the English abroad,
Fingers down a blackboard,
Spiders that run and hide,
Scary fairground rides,
Hairy legs,
Daddy-long-legs
Hail,
Snails,
Fetes,
First dates,
Yes these are some of the things we love to hate!

ThE HallOWe'En QuEeN

The Hallowe'en Queen is eighteen.
The Hallowe'en Queen is tall and lean.
The Hallowe'en Queen is black and green.
The Hallowe'en Queen is very mean.
The Hallowe'en Queen is rarely seen
The Hallowe'en Queen has almost gone
before she's been.
The Hallowe'en Queen
The Hallowe'en Queen,

She's a SCREAM if you know what I mean!!!

TuRniNg tHe TaBLeS

Me and my mate Pete built a bird table
That we thought was pretty neat,
To enable the birds to eat nice and neatly
Instead of having to eat at me and my mate
Pete's feet.
Which we both thought for the birds would be
A nice treat.
But much to our surprise the birds seemed
To prefer to meet, tweet (not on Twitter!)
And greet on the grass at our feet and on the
Bird table passed,
Which to me and my mate Pete, seemed daft.
And I know it sounds absurd but we both felt
The birds were giving us the bird!
Still me and my mate Pete had the last laugh
Because, boy is my cat fast!!

TiCkLeD PiNk

I new a grumpy salmon
Who rarely ever smiled
Until he met a funny trout
Who tickled him a while
He tickled him so much
He couldn't help but laugh
You could say the salmon was tickled pink
But that would be plain daft!

ThE PeRfEcT (G)HoSt

I don't want to boast
But living in my house
I've got the perfect ghost.
He can make the toast,
Cook the Sunday roast
He even collects the post
And he never gives up the ghost.
In fact as ghosts go you could say
He's the perfect (G)host!

ThAt's An ExAgGeRaTiOn SuReLy ?

'For heaven's sake don't exaggerate,'
My dad once said to me.
'Your baby brother hasn't got eyes as big as the moon.
You didn't wait an eternity for the bus
And your gran isn't one hundred and twenty three.'
Then one day as my dad came running past me
Shouting and screaming, 'Help me, help me, please
I'm being chased by a swarm of angry killer bees.'
I said 'Dad for heaven's sake don't exaggerate.
Yes, you are being chased by some angry killer bees
But twenty three killer bees hardly constitutes a swarm surely!'

GoiNg   FoR   COLd

If there was an Olympic gold medal for catching a cold,
Then I'd win every time.
If I'm on a train or waiting for the bus in the pouring rain,
I can guarantee I'll always be standing next to someone
Who's wheezing or sneezing, spreading their viral infection
In my general direction.
Never putting a handkerchief over their nose for my protection.
Yes, I wouldn't mind winning bronze or silver but if I had
A stinker of a cold I'm sure I'd win gold and then other
peoples colds wouldn't get up my nose,
In fact I'd welcome their germs but on my terms.
I've certainly done the training,
My nose has been running for weeks.
In fact it's running as we speak.
My head is splitting my throat is sore
And you should hear me moan and groan.
On that score alone I'm worth a gold medal I'm sure.
Well at least at the Winter Olympics.
That's if I'm picked and if I am then who nose
I just might win the gold medal for a cold, let's hope so!

ShArK AtTaCk iN ReVeRsE 2

A shark gets awfully bad press,
I wouldn't be surprised if it gets depressed.
I mean, hasn't it already got enough on its plate,
Being the creature we all love to hate.
So it's eaten a few of us, but how many of us have eaten
Shark and chips, so aren't we just a bunch of hypocrites.
And just think of all the shark merchandise we sell,
Do they get any profits? Do they hell!
And they say sharks have small beady eyes and just one look
Will scare a small child.
But it's not their fault the way they look and if you were a
Shark wouldn't you be scared of a great big hook.
So please give sharks a break,
And if you don't I'll put one in your bath and leave you
To your fate!
So don't berate them 'coz sharks are great.
(especially great whites!)
Shake one by the fin and let's have a shark love in.
Yes, lets put them on the list of things we love,
Instead of the list of the things we love to hate.
After all what have we got to lose ....
.................Apart from an arm or leg or two!!

It'S NOt WoRkiNg OuT So GeT OuT

How to deal with workers that are not performing.

Santa Claus - Give him his sack back and tell him he's sacked.
N.A.S.A. scientists - Give them a rocket.
Travel agents - Send them packing.
Chefs - Give them a good roasting.
Clock repairers - Give them a good ticking off and tell them next time they'll be clocking off permanently.
Journalists - Have a strong word with them.
Detectives - Tell them they haven't got a clue.
Athletes - Tell them to take a running jump.
Psychiatrists - I'd give them a piece of my mind.
Waste disposal contractors - Dump them.
Acrobats - Tell them to get their act together.
Hairdressers - Get them to cut out all the chat or you'll wash Your hands of them (I've been dyeing to do that one!)
Hit men - Just don't renew their contracts.
Rodeo riders - Tell them to buck their ideas up.
Ship builders - give them a stern talking too.
Police men or women - Read them the riot act.
Football managers - Send them for an early bath.
Librarians - Throw the book at them.
Croupiers - Tell them to collect their cards and go.
Waiters - Tell them to serve out their notice and then go.
Racing drivers - Get ride of them fast.
Gym instructors - Tell them they're not pulling their weight.
Yes, it's not working out so please just get out!

ChOcOLaTe RoCkS

Chocolate rocks, chocolate rolls,
And I know it costs,
But without it I'd be completely lost,
But a lot thinner and without so many spots,
And I know my teeth it rots.
But, so what, yes to me chocolate rocks!
Now if you don't mind leaving me in peace
So I can finish off the rest of this box!

RaiLiNg AgAiNsT JuNk MaiL

The postman puts so much junk mail
Through my door every year,
No wonder the rainforest
Has almost disappeared!

287

FrOm BaD tO WoRsE

I don't mean to be tearse
But there's nothing so bad
That it can't get worse,
With the exception of course,
Of the end of the universe!

A FuNnY ThiNg

Here's a funny thing
A caterpillar wants one final fling
Before it grows its wings!

ThE CAtS WhiSkErS

Cats WAIL when you stand on their tail
Cats HOWL when they're out on the prowl
Cats PURRRRRR when you stroke their fur
Cats clean and preen with their paws
Scratch their claws on all the doors
Yes, cats think they're the cat's whiskers that's for sure!

ThAT'S FRiGHTENiNG

A witch's teeth are really frightening
And frankly in need of some serious whitening!

SoMe DrEaMs ArE A NiGhTmArE

I've got nightmares stalking me.
Was it because I ate too much cheese for tea,
Or was it because last night I watched fright night
On DVD?

I've got nightmares stalking me.
Was it the rustle of the trees
Or watching *Most Haunted* on TV with eyes of
green and high pitched SCREAMS,
Even though there's nothing there to see.

I've got nightmares stalking me.
Oh why, oh why can't they leave me be?
I've really tried but I just can't flee
Yes' I've got nightmares stalking me.

Continued over the page:

I've got nightmares stalking me.
Ghostly, ghastly, beastly ghouls,
Vampires, werewolves, climbing walls.
Monsters, devils, hairy things,
Even dragons with great big wings.
Biting slashing at my neck,
No wonder I'm becoming a nervous wreck.

What's that – I thought I heard a SCREAM.
And I'm relieved to wake up to find this nightmare
Was simply just a DREAM!!

NOt A RhYmE AbOuT TiMe

Procrastination is the thief of time,
Which is a good line.
Pity I can't find a place for it in this rhyme,
But perhaps in another rhyme.
Maybe about calendars or diaries at a later date might work,
Or perhaps I could save it for another day.
Or maybe I could fit it into a poem about time travel
Or clocks or maybe not, who can say.
Maybe I could use it in a verse about rain
Or never making your mind up when or where
To go on holiday, and then trying to book it
But finding you've left it too late.
A bit like prevaricating in fact.
Anyway it's no good to me at this point in time
In this rhyme, so for the time being
I'd better put it away for a rainy day…………………….
…………………………………………….but then again!!

A MaRmOsEt As A PeT

Imagine if you bought a marmoset as a pet,
Only to find it had Tourette's.
Would you be upset to have been sold a pet
That had Tourette's, and then regret having bought
The marmoset from the outset?
Or would you sue and return the marmoset
And instead buy a gnu?
Or perhaps the fact that your pet Marmoset,
Could repeat the alphabet from A to Z,
Would quickly off set the initial regret,
And quickly you'd forget your pet had Tourette's.
After all it's pretty unique,
Having a pet that can speak,
Even if it does use the occasional colourful expletive
Wouldn't you agree.
Yes it's my bet that once you'd got to know your pet
Marmoset, you'd completely forget it had Tourette's,
And just be glad you had a marmoset as a pet
And not a gnu after all!

ThE TrOuBLe WiTh KeEpiNg ExOtIc PeTs

A condor is a bore and I'm sure keeping one in your house
Is almost certainly against the law.
An albatross, think of the cost.
A flea you'd lose to easily. Thinking of setting up a flea circus
Well if I were you I'd scratch that one off of your list.
I mean who would ever come to see it!
A poisonous snake would obviously be a big mistake.
A koala (bear) is far too much of a palaver.
A bandicoot although admittedly cute would soon scoot.
A great white shark don't be daft for a start you'd never get
It in your bath, didn't your ever watch *Jaws*?
A buzzard have you got a death wish wouldn't you be much
Happier with some tropical fish.
A grizzly bear, now be fair, it would be far too big to climb
The stairs and all that grizzling would have you tearing out
your hair!
A komodo dragon would be a fire hazard (health & safety!)
A giraffe are you having a laugh? A shark was bad enough!
An elephant? That's the most ridiculous thing I've ever herd!
A wildebeest, look just go away and leave me in peace.
A kangaroo? that's it I've had enough hop it!
A baboon? Look if you haven't got enough room to swing a
Cat you won't have enough room to swing a baboon will you?
A pride of lions or a man-eating tiger ? Come, come, have you
taken leave of what little sense you've got left or have you
been drinking and are seeing pink elephants again?
The trouble with keeping exotic pets debt and death and they're
Two pretty good reasons not to, wouldn't you agree!

ThE MaD PrOfEsSoR

Yes, I must confess, said the mad professor in his string vest
It was me that created that horrid looking mess on my desk,
And I know I look quite grotesque with my wind swept hair,
My ill fitting clothes and my tiny half moon spectacles
Perched on the end of my nose.
Yes don't you know I'm every inch the mad professor from
Head to toe.
And yes I must profess I rarely look my best,
Especially after falling asleep on my desk,
Reading the Times not the gutter press.
And it's true I am a little absent minded and often have to be
Reminded about tests I've set about Edward the Confessor,
To please some fastidious assessor.
And I must confess, said the mad professor, you'd never
Have guessed I had a first at Oxford and to see how much I
hoard in my study no wonder most of my students call me
An old fuddy duddy.
With my head always stuck in a book I often forget to cook
Or wash, I'm sure I must stink.
And some of my students, behind my back, or so I've heard
Unkindly call me the missing link.
Yes, I'm the mad professor and I must confess that's if you
Hadn't already guessed I really couldn't careless!

It'S MeAnT tO Be

Don't you see,
It's meant to be?
Like the birds and the bees,
The leaves and the trees,
The fish and the sea,
The legs and the knees,
The door and the keys,
And the dog and the fleas.
Yes, it's meant to be,
Like you and me
And if not then I guess I could always fit you up
With a zebra or a kiwi on a blind date for a small fee!

ThErE's An ALiEn iN tHe SuPeRMaRkEt QuEuE

There's a alien in the supermarket queue.
And he doesn't seem to know quite what to do,
In fact he hasn't got a clue.
Yes, there's an alien in the supermarket queue.

There's an alien in the supermarket queue.
And I think he feels like a bit of a fool.
Well, you would too, wouldn't you.
If you were the only alien in the supermarket queue?

There's an alien in the supermarket queue,
And it's beginning to create quite a hullabaloo.
He's tried jumping from line to line,
But he comes back to this one every time.
I think he's got a crush on the checkout girl
But I'm not quite sure. Yes, it's hard to tell.
The checkout girl just caught his eye
And gave our alien a great big smile.
Though it's hard to tell when an alien smiles
Because they've got three heads and a thousand eyes.

Continued over the page:

There's an alien in the supermarket queue.
And as the supermarkets due to close at noon,
If he's going to ask her out he better do it soon,
But the alien just walked out and never said goodbye
I think our alien was just a little too shy.
Perhaps he'll be in tomorrow and try once more
Once he's picked his little alien heart up off the floor.
And that's if it's not against any alien laws to ask a checkout
girl, of course!

WhO InVeNtEd tHe WhEeL?

Look I know it's no big deal, (not unlike the Wagon Wheel)
And I've tried googling it with zeal but get no answers
Or any that are real.
So I make this humble appeal,
Can anybody please tell me…………………………….

Who invented the wheel?

O   O

Imagine if you found out that somebody in your family tree
Had invented the wheel, what a big deal that would be.
Then you could contact the patents office and get the royalties
Back dated or if you prefer, retrospectively.
Then everybody in your family would be very rich indeed!

I'Ve GoT A BoNe tO PiCk WiTh YoU
(FuNnY BoNeS)

A skeleton's bones of contention: a bona fide list.

A skeleton hates playing football in the winter because the
Pitches are always so bone hard.

A skeleton hates the TV programme *Bones* for the title alone!

A skeleton hates anybody who makes a bone-crunching tackle
On them and when they do is prone to call them a bone head
Or numbskull!

A skeleton hates not having a pocket to put their skeleton keys
in. (May I suggest they put them in one of their eye sockets?).
A skeleton hates people coming up to them in the pub and
Saying 'I've got a bone to pick with you.' No, they don't find
That in the least bit funny or HUMUROUS!

A skeleton hates people accusing them of being bone-idle
Or a lazy bones or having skeletons in their cupboard.
And they hate riding in old cars they call them bone-shakers!
A skeleton hates getting into a fight with anyone.
They say they haven't got a bad bone in their body.
Personally speaking I don't think a skeleton's
Got the stomach for a fight or in truth much of a back bone!
A skeleton hates going down a bobsleigh run on a skeleton
sledge they say that scares them to death I'd never have
guessed!

Continued over the page:

A skeleton makes no bones about the fact they hate dogs
Coming up to them and licking them all over and trying to
Chew on them yes, that's definitely a bone of contention
For any self respecting skeleton, and over that one they won't
Let go with out a fight, you could say they're like a dog with
A bone or maybe not!

A skeletons hates any song with lines like, 'give a dog a bone'
Or 'them bones them bones them dry bones' and would have
A bone to pick with anybody who had one as a ringtone on
Their mobile phone.

A skeleton hates the wind because they say it goes right
Through them chills them to the bone and dries out their skin.

A skeleton hates pirate ships because of the pirate flag
The skull and crossedbones they hate pirates, they say,
Skulduggery isn't pleasant!

A skeleton hates it when it's hot especially at night as it
Makes their throat as dry as a bone.

Yes, a skeleton has got a lot to put up with, so give them a
break, after all they're very thin skinned,
especially about their weight!
Actually they're not they're bad to the bone!!
Right pick the bones out of that lot!!
And don't moan and groan about all the lame bone jokes
Or I'll have a bone to pick with U2 !
(I only hope Bono doesn't sue!)

BaTs iN tHe AtTiC

I know I'm acting quite erratic
And beginning to sound like I've got bats in the attic
But I can assure you that the study of coins and medals
Is called numismatics!

And if you don't believe me then I suggest you look
In the dictionary!

Try picking a word out of the dictionary and then writing
A nonsense rhyme
Though believe you me it's not always that easy
But if you have a problem with a word that won't behave
Properly send them over to me and I'll have a quiet word
In their ear metaphorically and then send them early to bed
Without any tea!
Especially if it's that word naughty, yes I've often found the
Word naughty behaving extremely badly being disobedient
Mischievous and unruly and hoity toity and those are only
The words I've picked out of my pocket dictionary!

A PoEm AbOuT TrYiNg tO WriTe A PoEm

I sit here pen in hand, waiting for the muse to strike.
Waiting for an idea that's right,
Something that will also rhyme I scribble something that
Makes no sense, something about the present tense.
Looking for some clever line but today
Nothing springs to mind.

Another page goes in the bin, another verse that won't fit in.
No play on words no clever rhyme is this scribe wasting
His time.

If I could find an opening line to start me off then I'd be fine,
Perhaps something about the missing link and something to
Really make you think.
Something witty clever too at this stage anything will do.

The harder I try the worse it gets this poem I think I should
Just forget.
My mind just won't get into gear it's like a black hole I fear.
Perhaps it would help me to think if I had a little drink
Oil the wheels then off I'd go, to help the creative juices flow.

But all I do is stare into space
The blank page I can no longer face.
So I think I'll retire to bed instead
Because it's not going to come as any great shock
I'm tired and suffering from writers block!

ReCyCLiNg My BiKe

I love to recycle things and put them in my
Recycling bin.
Things such as –
My rusty bike, my sister's favourite pink tights,
Some cans of coke,
A corny old joke,
A vampire's cloak,
A black hole, an empty loo roll,
Shoes,
Old news (so they can make it new!)
A feather (because it rhymes with the next line!)
The cycle of life so I can live forever!
Tins, sharks fins,
An empty bottle of gin,
The recycling bin!
Three wishes, my mum's dirty dishes,
Bubble gum,
Some currant buns (passed the sell by date)
My brothers bling,
An old broken 45 record by Elvis the King,
Yes, I love to recycle things and put them in
The recycling bin. (even things I shouldn't!)

A LeSsOn iN DePrEssiON

Has any one guessed that you're depressed or do they just
Think you're lazy or it's you age or you're just not doing
Your best?
My guess is the latter.
When you're depressed you don't chatter, you've lost your
Patter, nothing matters, you don't even clatter about anymore,
Your eyes are on the floor.
Your thoughts go deep, you can't sleep, you constantly weep,
You don't eat, people you no longer want to meet.
You feel like the proverbial black sheep.
You're filled with doubt, you want to shout but nothing comes
Out. Don't keep it inside or try and keep it at bay like King
Canute tried with the tide.
I know you're not in the pink but you're not the weakest link,
You're not alone, phone a friend, phone home.
Here's a lesson, one in four probably more, suffer from
depression sometime in their lifetime and some of those are
kids. Here's news, there's no shame, no one's to blame,
Get help and banish the blues then you can get back to doing
Whatever you want to do……..okay when I said whatever I
didn't mean you had to learn to play the didgeridoo, that's
Too much of a hullabaloo. Couldn't you learn to play the
triangle at school? Yes, that's cool!

SpiDeRs ArE CoOL

Spiders are cool
Spiders are fun,
Unless a red back
Bites you down under on the bum
Then as a rule spiders are not so cool
Or fun after all!

Spider note: A red back Spider lives in Australia and
Often hides out in the dunny (outside toilet)

WiZaRdS AnD WiTcHeS
(BiTcHiN' iN tHe KiTcHeN)

The witches got into quite a to-do
The night they tried cooking a wizard's brew.
In fact there was quite a hullabaloo, and the wizards
Threatened they were all going to sue.
The wizards said the witches hadn't a clue
And the witches' brew tasted more like a bad Irish stew
Than a wizard's magic brew.
The witches weren't cool about the whole ballyhoo
And into a rage they instantly flew.
The wizards were bitchin'
The witches weren't bewitching
And you've never seen such a mess in the kitchen.
The plates were flying the witches were crying
You could see on its feet the party was dying.
It all I'm afraid ended in tears,
When the witches and wizards all disappeared.
Together they created a magical spell
Which I've got to be honest didn't go well
And the witches and wizards then all ended up at
The bottom of a very deep wishing well,
Which created merry hell amongst the witches and wizards
Especially as the wishing well smelt like hell!
And the moral of this story is if you're a wizard or a witch
Try to get along or the magic spells you cast might just
Go horribly wrong!

WhO CaReS AbOuT tHe ThReE BeArS?

Who cares about the three bears?
Not me! After all they've got more than enough food
To feed three, even with Goldilocks coming over later for tea.
Yes, who cares about the three bears?
Certainly not me! After all they can't be that forlorn,
Their coats are nice and thick and warm.
Yes, these three bears don't know they're born.
Okay, so Goldilocks is coming round in the morn to eat
All their porridge, but they're bears for goodness sake.
So I don't mean to be rude but they can always forage
For some more food.
Who cares about the three bears? No, not me.
I've got enough to worry about with the credit crunch
Than to worry about what the three bears are having for lunch.
I mean what a bunch of losers. I can just imagine the three
bears down the local boozer the Dog and Duck bemoaning
Their bad luck. Yes, as far as I'm concerned the three bears
suck, grizzling and crying in their beer. If I were Goldilocks
I'd steer well clear.
Yes if I were Goldilocks I'd go and join Little Red Riding Hoodie
In the woods or go and visit the three little pigs in their new
Digs. Or she could always go and see Cinderella's new fella.
He's a right charmer or so I'm led to believe.
Anything's better than being around the three bears they're
Just so lame.
If I had my way I'd cover the three bears in honey and leave
Them in a room full of killer bees.
Yes, who cares about the three bears? Nobody, least of all me!

WhO Am I?

I shrink and don't grow
I love to pose and put on a good show
I can't blow my nose or feel my feet or toes
So who am I, do you know?

Answer: Yes that's right I'm a man made of snow!

ThE DiNoSaUr NeVeR SaW iT CoMiNg

The poor old dinosaur never saw the asteroid coming,
As the asteroid tore its way across the forest floor
The dinosaur gave one last almighty roar
And then the dinosaur was no more!

The dinosaur never saw the asteroid coming!
Obviously the dinosaur wasn't that bright or didn't have
Very good eyesight, anyway it's all too late now,
That will forever be the dinosaurs fate and fatal mistake
That it saw the asteroid far too late.
Anyway, can you imagine the chaos if the dinosaurs were
Alive today running up and down the motorway?
So I hate to say it but it was probably a good thing the
Dinosaur never saw the asteroid coming as I for one wouldn't
Fancy being ate by a great big dinosaur as it crashed through
My garden gate!

NOt SuCh HaRmLeSs AdViCe

They say shaking a cannibal by the hand
Is a fairly harmless thing to do,
But whoever said that hasn't got a clue,
Because if you do you'll end up armless,
Having got yourself into a right stew!

NOt SuCh A FuNnY BoNe

Frankenstein loves to moan
That he's got a funny bone.
Actually, he's got quite a few,
And none of them are his own!

ThE IdiOtS GuiDe tO FLyiNg A KiTe

One for maximum fun find a place where there's plenty of
room to run (I assume you don't own a mansion so
Obviously not in your living room, to do so would be lunacy
And if you did then I could only assume that later you'd be
howling at the moon too!)
Nowhere near a cliff would be high on the list of places to
Give a miss, unless you want to go hang-gliding on the cheap
Or you've got no fear or it's leap year!
Find a place where you feel at ease and is devoid of any large
Trees like oaks or redwoods.
And I don't mean to tease but the key to a good kite flying day
Is to make sure there's a good strong breeze.
Otherwise you're just going to get down when you can't get
your kite off the ground.
Be warned, if your kite contains metal struts, flying your kite in
A thunderstorm would obviously be nuts,
It also strikes me it would be extremely frightening if you got
Struck by lightning, so don't do it on this one,
There are no ifs or buts. (well it is the idiots guide and you
don't really want to get fried!)
Footwear is important, a comfortable shoe is a must, definitely
no clogs and never, fly your kite in a park full of dogs.

Continued over the page:

One because dogs chase things and two, look do I have to
explain everything too you. (Dogs number twos) you really are
New at this kite flying caper aren't you?)
Now you're going to fail if your kite hasn't got a very long tail,
But not too long please or you'll spend the rest of the day with
the tail wrapped around your knees.
String, make sure you've got some attached to your kite would
be my advice otherwise you're going to look a right
Charley running up and down with a kite stuck in your hand.
If you've got a red kite avoid any fields that might be inhabited
By a bull (surely nobody's that much of a fool!)
Get up a good head of steam and your kite should fly like
A dream.
Yes, if you abide by this idiots guide to flying a kite your kite
Flying days should be out of sight and a pure and utter delight.
Mind you not too far out of sight you don't want to interfere
With any passing satellites!

TwiTtEriNg On

Some people go twittering on and on and on
But those people don't belong on Twitter
Where a tweet that goes on too long
Is frowned upon!

A VaCuUm iN SpAcE

A Hoover is a bit like a black hole
In space,
It sucks everything up
And leaves a vacuum in its place!

I SpiEd A SpIdEr

I spied a spider in a spider's web in the garden shed
But the spider I spied in the spider's web in the garden shed
Was alas not alive but dead.
Still better the spider I spied in the spider's web
In the garden shed dead it should be said
Than alive and hiding somewhere in my bed!

WeAtHeR U LiKe iT Or NOt

Today it will probably be hot
And tomorrow there will be a lot more weather
Whether you like it or not!

NeVeR TrY AnD StOp A TrIcERaToPs

Never try and stop a triceratops
When it's at the local hop
Bopping `till it drops
`'Coz if you do it will get into a strop
Then blow its top
And you'll kop it
When it lands on you with a belly flop
In terror your eyes will pop
And then it will devour you
With its great big chops
Which will permanently put a stop
To your biological clock
So before you try and stop a triceratops
Bopping `till it drops at the local hop
My advice would be........................

Stop   you clot or that will be your lot!

I do hope now you've seen the error of your
Ways and the penny's finally dropped!

316

My ImAgiNaRy FriEnD

My imaginary friend Ben is someone on whom I can
Always depend.
He never drives me round the bend
And on Ben I can always depend to defend me
To the bitter end.
Ben will always be around, especially when I'm in a bind,
Come rain or shine.
Yes, when we're together me and Ben have a wonderful time.
My imaginary friend, Ben, never moans or groans
Or asks to borrow my mobile phone or taps me up for a loan
And with me never takes a sarcastic tone.
And when we go out for the day,
Ben will always let me have my own way
And let me have the final say on what games we play.
And Ben will always be there when I need him most,
Especially when I need someone to take the blame
For when I burn the toast!

A OnE LiNe RhYmE AbOuT A PoRcUpiNe

ThisisaonelinerhymeaboutsittingonaporcupineOuchyouswine!

Now you try and write a rhyme on one line let's face it
It can hardly be worse than mine!!

PoEtiC LiCeNcE 2

Being a poet
With words i'm a bit of a hoarder
And I like to use them
But not necessarily in the right order!

318

PaNdOrA's BoX

One day Pandora was browsing through an antique emporium
With her mother which was filled with a cornucopia of
Weird and wonderful delights.
When she came across a very small dusty looking box that
Happened to catch her eye.
To be honest it was nothing special but it was cheap and
Pandora didn't get a lot of pocket money.
So she bought it. On her way home she thought about the box
And how she wished it was bigger. Still, she thought,
I can put some jewellery, in it and when I polish it up it will
Still look nice on the dressing table in my bedroom.
Little did Pandora know what the unassuming looking box
Had in store for her, well you should always be careful what
You wish for and Pandora was about to find that out.
That night Pandora woke with a fright when she heard a knock-
ing sound which seemed to be coming from the direction of the
Dressing table. Pandora got out of bed and put the light on
And wiped the sleep out of her eyes, what little she'd had.
As she got closer to the dressing table much to her surprise
She realised the noise was coming from the small box she'd
Bought earlier that day at the antique emporium.
Nervously she opened up the lid of the box in fear of what
She might find. Perhaps the bogey man was hiding there a
voice inside her head cried.
On opening the lid she stared in disbelief to find that the box
was no longer small but big, extremely big.

Continued over the page:

The box was now like a deep well and on one side of the
Well was a ladder, Pandora's fear was now replaced with
Intense curiosity as to what was at the bottom of the well.
Pandora gingerly climbed down the ladder until she reached
The bottom rung and then jumped the last few feet onto the
Ground below.
Pandora shone her torch around the walls of the well.
She could see a corridor, so she slowly made her way along it,
As she did she could feel her heart pounding in her chest
But she couldn't stop now as she continued on Pandora came
Across the following things:

A grandfather clock (that went tick tock).
A Rastafarian with long dreadlocks.
Goldilocks, (minus the three bears) who was covered in spots
Presumably chicken pox.
An old wizened warlock playing on his X-Box.
A detective called Sherlock.
Some glowing moon rocks (I say moon rocks only because
There was a label attached to them stating that they were moon
Rocks, and to be honest Pandora had no reason to doubt there
Authenticity).
A baseball team called the Boston Red Sox.
A frock resplendently covered in rubies and emeralds.
A jockey on a horse called Mr Spock and a large battleship
That was in the process of being docked.
This was all a lot to take in for Pandora, she felt quite lost.
Perhaps this was all just a vivid dream or an extreme
Nightmare, *after all* Pandora thought *I did have cheese on toast
For supper before I went to bed.*

Continued over the page:

By this time Pandora had got to the end of the corridor
Where she had reached a door.
Before she had a chance to make up her mind whether to open
the door or not, at that very moment from behind the door
Came a loud knock,
So bravely Pandora opened the door she was extremely
shocked to see a rather large lion standing there.
When the lion saw Pandora it roared, lifted its paw and then
Poor old Pandora was no more!

The moral of this tale is, be careful what you wish for,
Or like Pandora you may well get more than you bargained for
And Pandora certainly got more than she bargained for!
Sorry if you were expecting a happy ending,
But it's no good pretending,
Life's not always full of happy endings!!

DoN't PaNiC !

Don't panic and fear the worst
If you're on a ship called the Titanic in a parallel universe.
It won't sink, or at least that's what I think.
Why, because in a parallel universe,
Everything's in reverse.

Don't panic if you're a bit part actor
In a parallel universe, and you're on the bridge
Of the Star Ship Enterprise,
And the Klingons take you by surprise
Because you won't die so enjoy the ride.

Don't panic if you're a vampire and you meet
Buffy the Vampire slayer, in a parallel universe.
There's no need to get uptight,
Buffy won't pick a fight and permanently turn out your lights.
She'll probably just kiss you goodnight (Alright Spike!)

Don't panic if you're a dinosaur in a parallel universe,
A giant asteroid won't wipe the floor with you
Of that I'm ninety nine point nine percent sure.

Continued over the page:

Don't panic if you're Little Red Riding Hood and you meet the
Big Bad Wolf in a parallel universe, he'll probably be good
And help you build a tree house in the woods.

Don't panic if you're opening up Tutankhamun's tomb
In a parallel universe you won't succumb to the curse.
Why?   Because you're in a parallel universe
And in a parallel universe everything's in reverse.
Mind you, I suppose that goes for the other way round too
James Bond, Superman, Harry Potter, Dr Who,
All you goody two shoes I'd panic if I were you!!

A ToNgUe TwiStInG RhYmE

Ten tiny tongue twisters standing in a line,
Twisting their tiny tongues around their tiny tonsils in time,
In this tongue twisting rhyme.
Until one dropped out and then there were nine.

Nine tiny tongue twisters standing in a line,
Twisting their tiny tongues around their tiny tonsils in time,
In this tongue twisting rhyme.
Until one dropped out and then there were eight.
(Which doesn't rhyme but never mind!)

Eight, seven six, five four, three,
Tiny tongue twisters standing in a line,
Twisting their tiny tongues around their tiny tonsils in time,
In this tongue twisting rhyme.
Until one dropped out and then there were two.

Two tiny tongue twisters standing next to each other
Twisting their tiny tongues around their tiny tonsils in time,
In this tongue twisting rhyme.
Until one dropped out and then there was one.

One tiny tongue twister standing on his own
Twisting his tiny tongue round his tiny tonsils in his own time,
In this tongue twisting rhyme.
Until he dropped out and then there were none.
One tiny tongue twister left surely that means he's won!
Thank goodness for that at last we're done!!

PLuTO YoU'Ve GOt 2 GO !

Some cosmologists were overheard to say the words
Damn it!
When they found out that Pluto had been reclassified
As a dwarf planet.
Personally speaking I don't know what all the fuss was about,
As far as I'm concerned Pluto only ever was
A Mickey Mouse planet!!

Cosmological Note:

Pluto was changed from a planet to a dwarf planet
By the International Astronomical Union in August 2006
Because it was deemed to be too small to be a proper planet.
Not all astronomers were happy about it.
The term 'Mickey Mouse' means small time or joke.
(But I'm sure you already new that and if you didn't what
  Planet have you been living on!)

WeReWoLvEs (NOt FoR tHe SqUeAmiSh)

Changing,
Maiming,
Muscle straining,
Wailing,
Impailing,
Blood staining,
Left human remainings,
The beasts not for taming,
Wall scaling,
Victims flailing,
Blood draining,
Scowling,
Howling,
Disemboweling,
Hairy, Scary, let's Bewary of the Werewolves
Or in truth the next victim could well be you!

ThEy'Re DrOpPiNg LiKe FLiEs

They're dropping like flies.
I wonder why they're dropping like flies.
Surely it can't come as any great surprise.
The reason why they're dropping like flies
Is because they're flies and when flies no longer fly
They drop from the sky and die
Hence the term they're dropping like flies, of course, 'I see,'
Said the venus flytrap whistfully, 'after all there are no flies on
me,' he added, unfortunately not having any frozen flies left in
the fridge for his tea.
I mean they're not dropping like elephants
And they're not dropping like bees or birds
Yes that would plainly be absurd
'They're dropping like flies,' said the spider to the fly,
With a huge sigh, as he waved the fly goodbye
But not before the spider,
Wide-eyed and not the least bit surprised, ate the fly
'That's put a fly in the ointment for the fly.' said the spider
His humour being extremely dry.
Then the spider feeling rather pleased with his debating skills,
Having just gone in for the kill,
Knowing he had just wiped the floor with the fly
Both physically and metaphorically then went back to his web
to hide,
Until another poor unsuspecting fly came flying by
Or dropped from the sky.
Yes, you're right this whole story is nothing more than a
Complete and utter web of lies, now there's a surprise!

DoN't ShOoT tHe BaNdiCOoT

A bandicoot is cute and quite a hoot
So don't shoot the bandicoot or hit it in your ute on route.
No, instead why not give it a toot and let it scoot
To play the flute or have some fun or lay in the sun?
Or maybe have a ride in a bobsleigh down the Cresta run
Before its day is done.
So don't be dumb, put away that gun,
Because a bandicoot needs its mum to stroke its tum.
So don't shoot the bandicoot, you old coot,
And lock it in your boot while you drink root beer.
Let is disappear.
No don't sneer, you wombat, do you hear
Or I'll be forced to put a boot up your rear!

Footnote: I fear the rabbit-eared bandicoot is getting closer
          And closer to extinction every year and like a
          Lot of animals will soon disappear.
          But after all it's only a bandicoot ……………..
          And who gives two hoots about the bandicoot!

A HulLaBaLoO At tHe LoCaL ZoO 2

There was a right old hullabaloo at the local zoo
And it's true it wasn't the first time there'd been a hullabaloo
At the local zoo hence the title a hullabaloo at the local zoo 2!
It all began one day when one of the zoo keepers flew into a
rage inside the tiger's cage and it took him an age to calm
down. Mind you he had just spent the night shut up tight inside
A tigers mouth without a bite to eat. Actually that's not strictly
True the tiger had opened up his mouth long enough for the
Zoo keeper to order a ham and pineapple pizza with extra
Cheese topping and some nice hot garlic bread, which did
Repeat on him a little and gave him a few nightmares, as if it
Wasn't bad enough being shut inside a tiger's mouth all night.
Now, to get back to the story. When the zoo keeper had calmed
Down, after hitting the roof, having stepped out of the tiger's
mouth when the tiger yawned which for the record was a sabre
Tooth (tiger that is)
The zoo keeper asked the tiger why he had kept him locked up
tight inside his mouth all night.
The tiger replied, 'well serves you right, now you know how it
feels to be locked inside a tiny smelly cage all day and night?'
The zoo keeper sympathised with the tiger's plight and
apologised and said, 'I think you're probably right.'
So later that day the zoo keeper let the tiger out of its cage
Which wasn't the brightest idea the zoo keeper had ever had.

Continued over the page:

The tiger, not having been fed that morning, probably due to
All the hullabaloo felt like a quick bite, so he had several.
In fact he ate everything in site including all the zoo keepers,
A rather angry gnu, an emu, who unfortunately had bird flu.
And all the birds in the bird house which included toucans,
Macaws and cockatoos who all got into a bit of a stew,
But when there's a tiger loose in your bird house there's really
Not a lot else you can do but get into a bit of a stew.
Yes, at this point I think it's fair to say there was one hell of
A hullabaloo at the local zoo.
Still, if you let a hungry tiger out on the loose that's what
hungry tigers are prone to do, eat you!
Anyway, to cut a long story shorter,
After the tiger had polished everybody off apart from the zoo
keeper because he had let him out of the cage,
There was now no longer a hullabaloo at the local zoo,
In fact there wasn't a single sound, not even a cuckoo, the
whole place was as quiet as a mouse,
especially in the bird house!
The zoo keeper who, once again, it has to be said, didn't have
the highest of I.Q.s decided as there was just him and the tiger
left at the zoo,
for something to do why not start up tiger rides
That could be fun.

Continued over the page:

Again obviously he hadn't thought it through fun, no fun,
It wasn't the whole idea was just plain dumb and soon the
children and their parents and the zoo keeper who, having tried
to run, all ended up inside the tigers tum!

The moral of this tiger's tale, which was told to me by an old
sage, is never try and take a tiger for a ride or you'll be in for
A nasty surprise,
And never keep a tiger in a cage at any stage or they'll
definitely be a hullabaloo at the local zoo, one and two!!

SpElLiNg BeE CoNuNdRuM

Question:

In a spelling bee what's the difference between the word
Do and the word don't ?

Answer:

In a spelling bee the difference between the word
Do and the word don't are the letter N and the letter T
And the apostrophe!

What's a conundrum ? That's a puzzle, No that's what it is
It's a puzzle a conundrum is a puzzle, next you'll be asking me
Something completely random like what's a panjandrum? …
A Panjandrum is a pompous person taken from a character
In a nonsense poem written by Samuel Foote in 1755
Are you happy now? GOOD!!

It'S nOt EaSy BeiNg A TreE

It's not easy being a tree, 'You're telling me
I'm absolutely freezing!' said the tree,
'Since I've shed all my leaves.'
So I went outside and gave the tree a nice hot cup of tea.
I can tell you the tree was so pleased.
I said to the tree, 'You looked so forlorn,'
The tree said 'I am,
It's not as if I can move around to keep warm.
I shall be so relieved to get my leaves back in spring,'
Said the tree, shivering and holding on with one of its branches
Tightly to the hot cup of tea.
I then went back inside feeling slightly guilty
That I was in the warm while the tree was still standing
Out in the cold looking forlorn and muttering under its breath,
'I don't know, these humans nowadays they don't know
They're born.
Without us there wouldn't be any air to breath.
Still,' the tree said reflectively, sounding a little relieved,
'At least I'm not standing in the rainforest.
I might be cold and bored
But at least I'm not lying on the forest floor
Having just been cut down by a chainsaw!'

YoU'vE GoT tO Be KiDdiNg Me

'You've got to be kidding me,' said the stoat to the goat,
Who was in the process of licking his coat.
The goat's voice horse from horsing around in a boat,
Said to the stoat, 'I kid you not I've got a frog stuck in my
throat!'
'A frog,' said the stoat, 'a frog, how on earth did you get a frog
Stuck in your throat?'
'Well,' said the goat, now no longer licking his coat,
'The only thing I can think of, however remote,
Is the frog must have jumped down my throat
When I ran into him in my boat.'
'Well, you old goat,' said the stoat, 'that really must have got
The frog's goat, you nearly running him down in your boat.'
'Well to be honest,' said the goat,
'If that's what actually happened then if I were the frog
And somebody nearly ran me down in their boat
It would almost certainly stick in my throat.'
'Me too,' said the stoat, trying very hard not to gloat.
'Well,' said the goat, 'my only hope is to apologise to the frog
And hope he gets fed up with being stuck in my throat.'
'Yes, that's your only hope,' said the stoat,
'But if I were the frog I'd be hopping mad that an errant goat
Had nearly run me down in his boat and I'd want to ram the
Apology down his throat,
Even if that meant I croaked as well,' said the stoat to his
friend the goat.

Continued over the page:

The goat now started to panic because he had started to choke.
Well you'd choke too if you had a frog stuck in your throat.
At that very moment the frog hopped out of the goat's mouth
A little green around the gills but seemingly none the worse
For wear and took a great big gulp of air,
As did the goat.
And when both the frog and the goat had suitably composed
themselves, the goat spoke,
But not before clearing his throat.
'I'm a fool and a stupid bumbling old goat to boot,
And other lamentations of similar ilk passed the goats lips,
And I couldn't be more sorry if I tried,' he cried drying his
eyes,
'And I didn't mean to run you down in my boat,'
He said to the frog, 'but my eyesight isn't what it used to be.'
'Well, I've got a good mind to frog march you down to the
Nearest police station,' said the frog, his eyes all agog,
'But I can see you're genuinely contrite and I can also see
You've got very poor eyesight.'
The frog knew this because all the time the goat was being
contrite he was actually addressing the stoat,
The goat was so relieved he could now breathe hugged the frog
But not before he had hugged the stoat who he had thought was
the frog, and not before the stoat had whispered in the goat's
ear that he was actually addressing him the stoat,
Then and only then did the goat hug the frog which brought
A lump to the stoat's throat and on that happy if rather
confusing note the goat the frog and the stoat got into the
goat's boat and sailed off down the river,

Continued over the page:

And as a dragonfly swerved athwart the currant,
The goat happily chuntering away to himself said,
'There's nothing as satisfying as messing about in boats.'
And it's true there isn't,
That is as long as the boats float.
Unfortunately half way down the river this boat didn't
And the goat the frog and the stoat all croaked because not one
of them could swim a single stroke,
Not even the frog as before when the frog got hit by the goat
In his boat he was wearing arm bands.
I'm only kidding that was a joke,
The goat the frog and the stoat all lived happily ever after
So happily ever after did they live in fact,
That now the goat dotes on the frog and the stoat
And the frog and the stoat both think the goat's a pretty good
bloke, although technically the goat's not a bloke, but a goat!
Although they did send the goat to an opticians to get a pair
Of spectacles,
Which the goat often broke on several occasions when he was
Messing around in his boat.
And when he did he'd break into more lamentations
And the stoat who was always more sanguine than the goat
Had to cheer him up with a joke.
And finally on that happy note that's all she wrote
About the goat the frog and the stoat (well almost!)
And you know after all that talking I think I might have got a
frog stuck in my throat, said the goat to anybody who might be
listening.

Continued over the page:

'You always have to have the last word don't you?'
Said the stoat. 'Yes I do,' said the goat,
'But unlike that bit about us all sinking in my boat,
This time in this rhyme that actually was a joke,
And quite frankly I thought it too be sublime.
That a joke,' said the stoat,
'You've got to be kidding me.
As a joke that wasn't worth a dime.'
'I kid you not,' said the goat determined to have the last word
On the very last line.
Unfortunately for the goat he didn't have the very last word on
the very last line the writer did when he said to the goat,
'I hope you don't mind but it's my rhyme and I'm having the
very last word on the very last line!'
And he also said to the goat,
'I hope you're not going to whine about not having the very
last word on the very last line because if you do
I won't include you in the sequel rhyme…………
You've got to be kidding me 2 !!'

WhY, WhY GoD
DiD YoU CrEaTe tHe CrAnE Fly

The daddy-long-legs vis-à-vis the crane fly
I ask, why God why, did you create the crane fly?
They make my little sister cry and every time I see one
I just want to run and hide.
So God, and I don't mean to be unkind,
But do you mind telling me why you created the crane fly?
Look, I can understand why you created the fly
As it cleans up germs or so I've recently learned.
So I say with a sigh why, God why did you create the crane
fly?
Were you bored inbetween creating the hippopotamus
And the giraffe and were looking for a little light relief,
Or at the time were you nodding off to sleep.
And I'm sorry God, I don't want to give you any grief
But it would be a big relief and a weight off of my shoulders
If you, God, could tell me why you created the crane fly?
Oh, and don't lie to me and I beseech you not to give me any
Of that all God's creatures and every living thing speech.
Okay fire away God, in your own time,
But sometime before Noah gets the ark out again would be
Good if you don't mind and you can spare the time,
And a window of opportunity opens in your busy schedule.
And as I crane my neck and look towards the sky God,
I ask why on earth did you create the crane fly?
As in the time it's taken me to write this rhyme
Another poor crane fly has been born, lived and died,
So God, why, why did you create the crane fly?

A BiG WuS

An octopus is a great big wus.
It never stands and fights.
It just takes flight and goes,
With its eight long legs in tow!

ThErE's NoThiNg To It

My next book will be entitled
The blank verses
2OO pages of blank verse written in invisible ink
Which should make the existentialists think!

Blank verse – Verse written without rhyme,
      Usually in lines of ten syllables

Existentialist – Philosophical movement stressing
      The personal experience and responsibility
      Of the individual, who is seen as a free agent.

Personally speaking I prefered the rhyme about the octopus!

HaViNg A WhALe Of A TiMe

I'm Horatio the humpback whale and today
I'm having a whale of a time chasing my own tail
So far as to catching my own tail it's all been to no avail
But one day, come rain shine or gale
I'm going to nail catching my own tail.
And when I do I'll really create a splash and everybody
Who sails past me will hail Horatio the humpback whale
As the only whale who can lick his own tail.
Yes, what a great tale that will be to tell my grandchildren,
Who will probably say, 'Grandad who are you trying to kid?
You're telling great big fibs,'
As they playfully dig me in the ribs.
Yes, I think you'll find especially in this rhyme
That Horatio the humpback whale is having a whale of a time!

ToP TeN ExCuSeS FoR NoT HaNdiNG YoUr HoMeWoRk iN On TiMe

1. I buried it in the back garden in my satchel
    In a time capsule.

2. I wrote my homework on rice paper and my sister Rachel
    Ate it, along with a nice hot chicken curry.

3. It just disappeared, 'Well yes Sir I suppose you're right
    Now I come to think about it I shouldn't have written it in
    Invisible ink.' they say with a wink!

4. It fell down the waste disposal unit in the kitchen sink.

5. I was ill but because I didn't want to fail I sent it by email
    You didn't receive it? Sir have you checked your computer
    For viruses lately?

6. Me and my sister got into a fight this morning just before I
    Set off to school and then she flushed it down the loo
    Your right Sir I might well have to sue!

7. A wizard turned me into a toad and only turned me back
    When I was hopping down the road, no Sir I'm not trying
    To goad you honestly.

Continued over the page:

8. A T-Rex fell through a time portal and ate it along with
    My brand new satchel this morning yes Sir that's right
    A woolly mammoth ate last week's homework,
    You've got a good memory Sir.

9. A strong wind came along and blew it out of my hand
    Straight into the tropical fish tank yes Sir I was surprised
    The piranhas ate it too!

1O. A burglar broke into our house last night and stole my
    Parents' antique desk the same antique desk coincidentally
    Where I left my homework in. Yes Sir it was lucky the
    Antique desk was heavily insured.

I'd be rather surprised if any of these creative excuses
Pulled the wool over a teacher's eyes
But you've got to admire the kids who are willing to try!

WhAt CaMe FiRsT tHe ChiCkEn Or tHe EgG ?

I said to my teacher
'Sir, what came first the chicken or the egg?'
Having been unable to find the answer on the world wide web.
My teacher looked down at me (well he was six foot three)
And, with an air of superiority, said to me.
'Well it must be the chicken, it can't possibly be the egg
surely?'
'Well,' I said, 'then Sir how come last Easter first thing in the
Morning I got an Easter egg and then later that day I had
Chicken for my tea?'
My teacher looked at me and frowned but nothing came out
Of his mouth not a sound,
He then turned round with egg all over his face and walked
Away. That took the wind out of his sails.
I thought *I bet a penny to a pound the next time I ask him a*
Question like that he chickens out.
Mind you, I also bet the next time I do a test in class I fail!
In anycase I blame my mate he was the one who egged me on
In the first place!

343

ThE TrOuBLe WiTh A SuiTcAsE
(An OpEn AnD ShUt CaSe)

The trouble with a suitcase is, it never knows when
To pack it in.

The trouble with a suitcase is, it doesn't know when to
Shut up.

The trouble with a suitcase is, it never knows whether it's
Coming or going.

The trouble with a suitcase is, it just doesn't know its place.

The trouble with a suitcase is, at times its full of itself.

The trouble with a suitcase is, it sometimes gets easily
Carried away. (But most of the time it doesn't!)

The trouble with a suitcase is, it often gets unfairly labelled
As a fly by night.

The trouble with a suitcase is, and I don't want to burst its
bubble but it takes flight at the first signs of trouble.

The trouble with a suitcase is, it just carries around too much
baggage with it.

The trouble with a suitcase is, search me I've got no idea!

344

ThE WiZaRd tHe WiTcH AnD
tHe RaT UnDeR tHe HaT

'I don't mean to cast aspersions,' said the wizard,
Casting aspersions, 'but as far as I can tell, someone
Around here smells like they've fallen down a rather
dirty smelly wishing well.'
'Well don't look at me,' said the witch, wanting to
dispel the wizard's aspersions right off the bat.
'Before I came out this evening I put on some
Channel No. 5 which for a witch is the equivalent of
an enchantment spell, and if I do say so myself,
I think I look rather bewitching.'
'I would have thought you could tell that,'
Said the witch, making a brew ha ha and creating
all kinds of merry hell, actually it was only one kind of
merry hell but I think all kinds of merry hell sounds so
much better don't you?
You could tell by now the wizard was really getting
on the witch's wick.
'Are you sure its not you that smells?' said the witch.
'That's rich,' said the wizard.
'The last time I saw you, you were face down in a
muddy ditch being violently sick having just fallen off
your own broomstick.'
'I resent that,' said the witch, 'You should be careful
About making accusations, after all mud sticks.'

continued over the page:

345

But the wizard wasn't convinced and persued the
matter rather vigoriously.
'Are you sure it's not you?' repeated the wizard,
Holding his nose in such a manner that made it fairly
Obvious he didn't believe the witch's protestations.
'I've got a feeling thou doust protest too much,'
The wizard continued, sounding extremely pompous
And looking as if he had got a bad smell under his
nose, which he obviously had!
That really made the witch's blood boil.
Which also, unfortunately for the witch, brought
several nasty boils to the surface of her already
sallow unpleasant complextion.
Things between the wizard and the witch had now
Turned extremely nasty indeed, in fact I would go
As far as to say they had got into a full blown spat.
The witch now seething with anger spun round
several times doing a rather good impression of a
whirling dervish and then with all her might threw a
kick in the wizard's direction.
Unfortunately for the witch, she hadn't put her specs
on that morning.
The wizard gave a quick shimmy, not unlike that of
the great wizard of the football pitch Cristiano
Ronaldo, and avoided the witch's boot with
relative ease leaving the witch down on her knees.
The wizard hardly batted an eyelid.

Continued over the page:

The wizard gave out a hearty side splitting belly laugh which to the prone witch seemed to last an eternity.

'Drat,' said the witch feeling rather foolish at her feeble attempts to get one over the wizard.

The wizard then finally went too far.

'You miserable cantankerous smelly old WITCH,' He said.

The witch was now even more angry so angry in fact she was spitting blood, although that could have been because she had broken one of her teeth in the fall and actually was spitting blood!

'Take it back, take it back,' said the witch flapping around like a demented bat.

'All you wizards are the same a repugnant lot of self satisfied toads, spat the witch, and as she did, Out popped the tooth.

The witch was now so flustered she had resorted to childish name calling.

'You smell, you smell, may you rot in hell.'

This, unbeknownst to the witch, was a very primitive name calling spell and instantly turned the wizard into a rat.

The witch shouted at the wizard, 'Wou dirty rat. Well what do you think about that?'

Continued over the page.

347

The wizard who was now a rat didn't hear this because he was stuck under his own rather pointy wizard's hat which had fallen off of his head and had slowly fluttered down and landed on top of him,
Leaving him trapped.
The witch caught herself thinking *howzat for a neat hat trick?* but tact prevented her from saying that.
I smell a rat, the wizard thought, not knowing just how close to the truth he actually was.
The witch felt justice had prevailed and did a slightly embarrassing jig around the wizard's hat, cackling loudly to herself, and singing 'The wizard's a rat, the Wizard's a rat, keep it under your hat but the wizard's a rat.' After she repeated that several times she then broke out into a few choruses of *I wish it could be Xmas Everyday* by Wizzard and then proceeded
To badly whistle the *Bewitched* theme tune
And after all that, that as they say, was the end of that! ....well again, not quite,
A few days later the witch, feeling the wizard's humiliation was now complete,
Decided too delete the spell she'd put on the Wizard all-be-it by accident rather than by design,
And turned the wizard back. With the aid of her new laptop, after doing a quick spell check!

Continued over the page:

'These computers are a whiz,' chortled the witch,
'Yes, it's so much easier for a witch these days than
having to make all those brews or potions or repeat
long incantations or enchantment spells,
And all that mumbo jumbo waving some twig
about,'
(by that she meant a wand!)
That's so passé and uncool and old hat!
These days if a witch wanted to put a hex on
somebody she'd do it by text!
Anyway, where were we, oh yes, the witch was just
in the process of turning the wizard back ....
But not before the rat, who was in fact a wizard
who'd been turned into a rat, had gone rat-a-tat-tat
on the side of the wizard's hat, no, not before that,
but after that.
Then and only then did the witch turn the wizard
back, who then scurried off with his tail between his
legs feeling like a bit of a rat having got into the spat
with the witch in the first place........................
And that really was the end of that.
I hope you managed to follow all that!
You didn't, well heaven help you when it comes to
Sitting your SATS!!

H A T S

I collect hats.
I have lots of them in fact.
Big ones,
Small ones,
Naff ones,
Cool ones,
Hats worn at school,
Hats that break the rules,
Hats worn by clowns,
Hats worn by the man about town,
Hats with corks,
Hats for sports,
Hats stolen (keep that one under your hat!)
Hats bought.
Soft hats, hard hats, sun hats, party hats, top hats,
Bowler hats, cricket hats howzat for a lot of hats?
All of which hang on my hat rack.
Hats, hats, hats, hats, so many hats they're driving me bats!
Hats worn to hunt
Or by baseball players who bunt
Or by rappers worn back to front,
Or by university students who love to punt.
Hats worn out in the sun or worn when you're out on the run
Right that's it no more hats I'm done!

(If you can think of any more hats than that
  Then I take my hat off to you!)

COmPLetE PaNDeMONiUM

There was complete pandemonium at
New York's Smithsonian when an extinct
Dinosaur interrupted a palaeontologists
Symposium playing an antique euphonium on
the floor.
What do you mean you don't believe me?
It's not like I've ever led you up the Garden
path before!
I have three hundred and sixty four times
Before are you sure?
Well I would like to say it won't happen
Anymore but it will of that I'm almost ninety
nine point nine percent sure!!!

BiRdS Of A FeAtHeR DoN'T ALwAyS StiCk tOgEtHeR

To be frank a vulture isn't a very cultured bird,
Or so I've often heard.
You'll never see one at the opera or looking round
An art gallery or at the ballet.
No, that would just be absurd.
For a vulture or so I've heard is much happier
Picking over the bones of some dead carcass and having
The final word.
On the other hand a little bird told me that another bird,
The condor, loves to study the law.
Along with the bald eagle who is extremely regal
And would never ever consider doing anything illegal I'm sure.
Yes, most birds of a more cultured nature would much rather
Pray in church, than sit on a perch and listen to some
Inane chatter (or tweet on Twitter) , to pass the time away.
Yes, birds of a feather do tend to stick together,
But not always I'd have to say!

ThAt'S NoNsEnSe

Some expressions don't make any sense
Like there's not enough room to swing a cat.
Well you'd think the R.S.P.C.A.
Would have something to say about that!
Or, that's a different kettle of fish.
Why would you want to put fish in a kettle?
Wouldn't it be better to put them in a dish.
Or, you're to slow to catch a cold.
Why would you want to catch a cold unless
You were in a cold research centre
And you were paid to do so?
Or, too many cooks spoil the broth
Why would you want to put any cooks in the broth
Unless you're a cannibal of course?
Yes, if you ask me some expressions don't make any sense.
But then again a lot of things don't make any sense
When you're only three!
But believe you me a lot of things don't make any sense
When you're forty three either just you wait and see!

BrOnTe tHe BrOnToSaURuS

This is the story of Bronte the brontosaurus
And how she loved to bore us
With tales of dragons that roar and chasing
Wild boar.
Playing hide and seek and making lame jokes
Like you never sarus or snoring and waking
Us all up with the dawn chorus.
And scraping her claws on all the cave doors
And picking thorns from out her paws
Or reading the stars out loud
Be it Leo, Pisces or Taurus.
And setting our nerves on edge by chasing
Baby woolly mammoths and nearly falling off
A cliff ledge.
Until one day Bronte the brontosaurus saw
A rather large stegosaurus and then poor old
Bronte the brontosaurus was no more us!
And that's the story
Of Bronte the brontosaurus
Admittedly it's pretty porous
But you haven't heard my story about
Waldolf the walrus
Now where did I put that thesaurus?

NeVeR FeAr ShAkEsPeArE

I plead don't be put off by Shakespeare the bard
And think he's too hard to read,
Shakespeare has planted the seed
For everything we read.
Old Will has written some cracking nonsense rhymes
With great lines like
Double, double toil and trouble:
Fire, burn; and cauldron bubble.

I think if Shakespeare was alive today what a great
sonnet he could write about the Hubble telescope.
Yes, what scope he'd have and I'm sure he'd think
Rap music was dope and would love Tu Pac's rhymes
And I wouldn't mind betting he'd have a laptop like
mine and be on Twitter all the time.
And he'd be surfing the net and I wouldn't mind
betting he'd have a duck-billed platypus as a pet!
Quill and ink he'd probably think.
Boy if I had a lap top back then I could have got my
Plays and rhymes written in half the time,
Still at least we didn't have global warming back then
Just the black death and the plague. Still at least
they're still performing my plays live on stage!

355

ThiNgS KiDs WiSh HaD BeEn InVeNtEd

A magic spelling bee that could whisper the correct answer in
your ear and disappear before anyone could see.
A Wii you could control by using your knife and fork while
you're eating your tea.
A wishing well,
Their own personal school bell they could ring whenever they
were feeling unwell, like a wizard doing a magic spell.
A giant chocolate bunny,
An endless supply of pocket money (don't be funny!)
A machine that could do all their homework.
A device so when you were being chased by a bunch of bullies
You can shout out 'Beam me up Scottie' like Capt Kirk.
A machine that could make sense of your dreams
A machine so you never had to take a bath or a shower but still
Managed to keep you clean!
A machine that could help you do well in your SATS.
A machine that could make you an amazing guitarist in five
seconds flat.
An invention that could get you out of detention
If I were a teacher that one I certainly wouldn't mention!
A time machine
A fuel that all cars use which is environmentally green.
A magic wand
Or an invention to make an endless supply of stink bombs.
Mind you if you invented a magic wand, it would make all the
other inventions redundant before too long!

MoNsTeR SelLiNg BiOgRaPhY's

Frankenstein: Stiched Up (Parts 1,2,3,4 & 5!)

Dracula: Biting Remarks SUCK!

Dr Jekyll: On A Hyding tO Nothing

Mr Hyde: My Ever Changing Moods.

Saskatchewan (Big Foot) ....Baby Steps

The Loch Ness Monster: I'm Not A Monster!

King Kong: Monkeying Around.

Godzilla: Who are you calling an Old Dinosaur.

Alien: I'm Not a Predator!

Predator: I'm Not an Alien!

The Hunchback of Nostradam: Standing Tall

A. Werewolf: A Change is as good as a rest.

Shrek: A Giant Among Men.

A. Zombie:....Dead on my feet

   All books available on Bad books dot. Con.
   (that's a Monsterous lie!!)

357

WhAt On EaRtH ArE We DoiNg
tO PLaNeT EaRtH?

I say this without a hint of mirth
And trying really hard not to curse
But what on earth are we doing to planet Earth?
If I were an alien I'd give us a wide berth!

GLoBaL WaRmiNg

Global warming is quite appalling
In fact it stinks
And I say this without a wink
But the human race
You are the weakest link
GOODBYE!!
(That might be our fate if the governments
of the world don't wake up before it's too late!)

PLaNeT EaRtH

From the sublime to the absurd
From an elephant to a bird
That's the evolution of our planet Earth.

FiRe(DoN'T)WoRkS!

As it starts to drizzle and the fireworks splutter
And fizzle out the kids mutter under their breath
And shout and the fireworks end up in the gutter
Or in the back garden as clutter
And if I'm ever going to get them to work
I think I might have to enlist the services
Of Capt. James T. Kirk!

ThE ToMBoY

The tomboy playing with the boys,
Making all the noise,
Breaking all the toys.
Sometimes can be coy
Often she annoys
But always a fathers pride and joy
Who would like nothing more
Than to be a boy called Roy!

ThE WiTcH iS WiCkEd

The witch is wicked the witch is cool
The witch is even magic at pool
And when skateboarding at the local mall
She makes all the young wizards drool
So you better accept her warts and all
Or you'll be heading for a massive fall.
Her teeth are yellow her teeth are black,
And inbetween each one a gap.
And best of all this witch can rap
In her back to front baseball cap.
The witch is wicked the witch is cool
The witch is the greatest of them all
And she's a wizard at football too
Yes the Wicked Witch is nobody's fool.
And that's the graffiti on all the walls
Of the Witches and Wizarding Witchcraft schools!
(Actually the witch isn't wicked or cool she's just a silly old
fool, who walks around all day long in a silly black pointy hat
carrying a broomstick under her arm wearing a black sheet!
To say the witch is wicked or cool is a bit like saying Santa
Claus can rap and what he carries around in his sack is wack!
Mind you I hope the witch doesn't read this or I just might
find myself climbing the beanstalk along with Jack!!
I also hope Santa doesn't read this either or I might not
get any presents this year for Xmas!!)

WhO StOLe SuE's DiDgEriDoO ?

Somebody stole Sue's didgeridoo from a didgeridoo do in
Timbucktu, but who?

Was it the emu? Or was it the kangaroo?

Or perhaps it was neither the emu or the

kangaroo but the gnu who stole Sue's

didgeridoo from the didgeridoo do in Timbucktu.

Either way Sue was so mad she wanted to sue

but who would Sue sue even the police hadn't got

a clue who had stolen Sue's didgeridoo from the

didgeridoo do in Timbucktu?

The emu blamed the kangaroo, the kangaroo blamed the

emu, the gnu blamed the kangaroo and the emu and said

they were both in cahoots.

Either way everybody had gotten themselves into

a right to-do over who stole Sue's didgeridoo from the

didgeridoo do in Timbucktu.

Continued over the page:

Then the emu flew at the kangaroo and told him
he was giving him bird flu which served him right for
jumping to the wrong conclusion and
blaming him for stealing Sue's didgeridoo from the
didgeridoo do in Timbucktu.
Then all hell broke out when the gnu joined in and all
three, the emu, the kangaroo and the gnu
got into a massive blue over who stole Sue's didgeridoo
from the didgeridoo do in Timbucktu.
The police had to admit it was a real puzzle and as a
puzzle it was harder to solve than a sudoku
was to do and after cross questioning them all
the police were forced to admit they still hadn't got the
slightest clue over who stole Sue's didgeridoo from the
didgeridoo do in Timbucktu.
The emu, the kangaroo, and the gnu having argued 'til
they were all blue in the face decided
to give it a rest and start a barbecue especially
as the kangaroo had started to Attishyooo!
After the emu had given him bird flu.

Continued over the page:

Then thankfully for this story….right on cue
into view came a shoe salesman from Peru who had
taken a photo (and put it on You Tube) showing quite
clearly that the emu, the kangaroo and the gnu had all
colluded in stealing Sue's didgeridoo from the didgeridoo
do in Timbucktu and had been pretending all the time
that they hadn't a clue what had happened to Sue's didgeridoo.
All three caused a ballyhoo when they were taken away
in handcuffs and put behind bars in the nearest available
zoo in Timbucktu.
Sue said thank you to the shoe salesman from Peru for
helping to catch the culprits in this
darstadly do then Sue proceeded to get a good solicitor so
Sue could sue the emu, the kangaroo and the gnu for
every penny they had,
which in truth wasn't that much, but Sue said
'Well it will just have to do.'
Then Sue went back to playing her didgeridoo
at the didgeridoo do in Timbucktu. Well if you
Could play the didgeridoo, wouldn't you?

A WaStE Of SpAcE

Black holes, empty loo rolls.
Igloo's in Kartoum,
A bassoon,
Parking spaces on the moon,
A clanger, an empty aircraft hanger.
A broken alarm clock,
One odd sock,
A millionaires money box.
A ghost rider, the Hadron Collider.
A haunted castle,
A footballers metatarsal.
The universe, an empty purse.
Zoo's, on a space station outside loos
Air pie, a crane fly.
The three-legged race
To anyone wearing false teeth, toothpaste.
Yes all these things are a complete
And utter waste of space!!

ThE BeSt DrEsSeD CrOcOdiLeS
On tHe RiVeR NiLe

Crocodiles can be very snappy dressers,
Especially in their crocodile shoes
And love to impress and look their best but
Can get very depressed and unhappy after
They've spent a night on the tiles somewhere
along the River Nile
And the next morning their clothes look a mess
And they have trouble using the trouser press.
I must confess I would never have guessed
That crocodiles got depressed because their
clothes looked a mess.
I just thought they couldn't care less how they
dressed and liked to look a mess like a lioness
Or Nessie the monster who lives in Loch Ness!
Bless (their little cottons socks.)
Yes it seems to me the best dressed crocodiles
with style by a mile along the River Nile…
smile.
Or is it just because they' ve had a feast?
Devouring a wildebeest and like showing their
teeth the vile beasts!

I FoUnD A WhiSpEr iN tHe ScHoOL PLaYgRoUnD

Please don't spread it around but yesterday I found a whisper in the school playground.
I said please don't spread it around but yesterday I found a whisper in the school playground!
No, not a blister, a whisper.
No, I didn't say I kissed my sister.
I said I found a whisper in the school playground, the school playground.
A Whisperrrrrrrrrrrrrr!!
I found a whisper in
The schoooooooool
playground!!!

Continued over the page:

No, it wasn't a chinese whisper I found in the school playground!

Sorry Miss I didn't mean to shout but I heard a whisper that shouting and mucking around will soon be banned in the school playground.
The teacher said, 'It's no longer a whisper and you've just earned yourself a week's detention for shouting and mucking around in the school playground!!'
So kids let that be a lesson to you, in future when you're in the school playground and you're playing and mucking around try not to make a sound!!

Yeah right like that's going to happen who are you trying to……Kid!!

MOsT HaUnTeD

Disappointed there are no ghosts in this rhyme
Most haunted look don't myther
There are no ghosts on TV's *Most Haunted* either!
In my house ghosts recently taunted
Why don't they rename it least haunted?
Because we're never on it!!

MaTcH AbAnDoNeD

Referee's match report:
(from the Twilight Stadium in Transylvania)
This was a fierce local derby with a lot at stake,
between Vampire Utd. And Vampire Slayer City
but I felt I had no choice but to abandon the
game due to the following.
One, I lost count of the number of biting tackles
that were flying in all over the pitch especially
from the Vampire Utd. Capt. Dracula.
Two, there were a group of Vampire Slayer City
supporters behind the Vampire Utd. goal that
were deliberately trying to put the Vampire Utd.
goalkeeper off by waving a cross in his direction
every time the ball came into his area, and
throwing cloves of garlic onto the pitch, and I
know vampire goalkeepers aren't that
comfortable with crosses at the best of times.
And three, players on both sides were constantly
fighting and at each others throats so in the end
I had to give all 22 players and managers the red
card and send them off for an early blood bath!
Match Referee: I.M. Squeamish.

A WiZaRd Of A ToNgUe TwiStEr

The wicked wizened wizard waved his
wicked wizard's wand at the wicked witch's
Wicket in a wicked game of cricket
But who was the wicked wizened wizard
Who waved his wand at the wicked
witch's wicket in their wicked game of
cricket which blew the witches wicket into
the thicket? Was Walter the Wizard?
Was the witch Wanda?.............either way
Both questions should make you ponder.
Whoever the wicked wizened wizard was
who was waving his wand at the witch's
wicket he obviously was not all the ticket!
Either way a wicked witch who loses her
wicket in a game of cricket is likely to
wave her own wand and expel the wizard
into the thicket along with the witches
wicket which just isn't cricket or is it?

ThiNgS ThAt SUCK!

Getting into a ruck with a Vampire,
Bad luck like forgetting to duck and getting hit
In the head with an ice hockey puck!
For your grandad losing his false teeth!
School semolina Yuk! (Yeah suck it up!!)
Having to work in the school tuck shop.
Living in the country and falling in some muck
Or being awoken by chickens that cluck.
For a chicken being plucked,
Well serves you right for all that clucking!
Being stuck on a bronco that bucks!!
A vacuum cleaner that sucks!
The end of the school holidays that sucks too.
Being the Shakespeare character Puck in a school
Play and forgetting your lines,
I think that's what they call being dumb-struck!
Being bossed around by Lord and Lady Muck.
Vampire bats. Repeats, cough sweets.
Breaking your arm, missing an episode of *Charmed*.
For Dracula sleeping in an uncomfortable tomb,
Being horror-struck by bad vampire's in *Eclipse*
Or *Twilight's New Moon*, tidying up your bedroom.
Yes with things that SUCK good luck
Now watch out for that ice hockey puck!!

EvERYbODY'S MaD AbOuT VAMPiReS BUT Me!

Everybody's mad about vampires but me.
Personally speaking I think anybody who's
mad about vampires is completely crazy.
And if they ask me how I feel about
Vampires i tell them they suck and I'm off
home to watch *Buffy the Vampire Slayer* on
DVD.
Everybody's mad about vampires but me
These days they're never off the TV in fact it
seems to me they're on TV more than *W.W.E.*
Yes vampires as far as the eye can see even
more vampires than witches and wizards
Playing around with alchemy.
What next vampires in 3D as if it isn't bad
enough watching them in HD!
Everybody's mad about vampires but me
Don't you see they're just a pain in the neck
speaking metophorically.(and literally!)
Everybody's mad about vampires and say so
should I be I say if they know what's good for
them they should just leave me be.

Continued over the page:

Everybody's mad about vampires but me
and because I'm not go batty and fly off the
handle and want to get into a fight.
So I turn around throw back my black cloak
show them my teeth and say 'BITE ME!'
Everybody's mad about vampires but me
I've got more sense I'd rather be stung by a
killer bee or be playing on my Wii or be
watching *Spooks* on the BBC or paddle in
the Dead Sea or and not wishing to incur
Anyones roth dress up as a goth and repair
my P.C.
Everybody's mad about vampires but me
Don't you see if you went to a restaurant
With a vampire they wouldn't order a blood
rare steak they'd order the waiter or you or
Me with a nice bottle of chianti!
Everybody's mad about vampires but me
but believe you me if you new that I was a
Vampire who was out for blood 'coz i
haven't had my tea then you wouldn't be
mad about vampires no Sireeeee!!
Now please leave me be so I can listen to
The Killers or Vampire Weekend on my MP3?
Yes everybody's mad about vampires.......
.....................................BUT ME!!

As PLeAsEd As PuNcH

As I sit here eating this sparse lunch
I'm as pleased as punch
I've just written a poem
About the credit crunch!

WhAt's LoUdEr ThAn A VuVuZeLa?

What's louder than a vuvuzela?
The battle cry of Vlad the Impaler?
The simultaneous sneezing of the whole
Population of Venezuela?
A drunk sailor singing through a loudhailer?
An American action film trailer?
Eric Clapton playing lead guitar on Layla?
Being scared by a spider if your name's Michaela?
A whaler getting hit by his own harpoon……..
Shouldn't that be a WAIL...ER!
What's louder than a vuvuzela?
Nothing, nothings louder than a vuvuzela
ABSOLUTELY NOTHING and that's official!!

A BiG HullabaloO!

HullabaloO

Yes it's true I may have over used the word
HullabaloO but what's it got to dO with
you?
If you don't like it I suggest you take a long
Walk to Timbucktu where you can listen to
Sue
Playing her didgeridoO at the didgeridoO
dO.
I think she's learning to play the vuvuzela
too
Now that really is a HullabaloO!!!

ThE LaSt ReSoRt

I wanted to be an astronaut
But I don't like confined spaces so that idea I had to abhort.

I wanted to be a psychiatrist
But decided not to, having given it much thought.

I wanted to be a maths teacher
But after my final report at school the idea came to nought.

I wanted to be a professional athlete
But unfortunately I'm not very good at sport.

I wanted to be an acrobat
But from my family I didn't get enough support.

I wanted to be a clock maker
But after thinking it over for a minute I had second thoughts.

I wanted to be a jewel thief
But I was afraid of getting caught.

I wanted to be a hotel manager in the Antarctic
But only as a last resort.
Unfortunately this is the last resort
Oh how I wish I was good at sport!

HaRrY ThE OtTeR AnD
ThE PhiLoSoPhEr'S RiNgToNe

Once upon a rhyme, not so very long ago,
There was an otter called Harry, Harry the otter.
And in this rhyme Harry inhabited a magical world
Full of weird and not so wonderful things.
(Bling being one of those not so wonderful things!)
Oh, and one more thing I should probably tell you,
Harry was a wizard but not a good wizard like certain
Other wizardy goody two shoes I could mention
But an absolute twenty four carat rotter of a wizard
otter.
But to be fair Harry wasn't the rottenest apple in the
wizarding fraternity not by a long shot.
That rather dubious honor fell to a weasel called
Vulgermort a vile wizard of such dastardly dastardliness
It made him feared and loathed in equal measures.
Actually in truth the measures weren't exactly equal it
was more like 55% fearing and 45% loathing but
whatever the measures were Vulgermort certainly was
despised throughout the wizarding world.

Continued over the page:

Vulgermort was suppose to have died in a freak
skateboard accident but some people weren't
convinced of this and thought Vulgermort was out
there somewhere just waiting to make a grand wizardly
Entrance at the drop of his crooked wizard's pointy
hat.

Nobody was suppose to mention Vulgermorts name,
Such was the fear it instilled in everyone.

So witches and wizards goblins, giants etc would instead
Say when referring to Vulgermort........you know him!
Everyone was acutely aware of the lengths that
Vulgermort would go to, to get one over on Harry and
anybody that attended Bogwarts, whether it be by fair
means or foul. One of those fowl times involved a
rogue chicken with bird flu that was found in the
grounds of Bogwarts which everybody was sure was the
handy work of Vulgermort but all ended well when the
chicken was caught and made into a nice tasty chicken
and asparagus soup, well when I say it all ended well I
of course do not include the chicken in the afore
mentioned all, for the chicken I'm afraid it all ended
extremely badly!

Harry attended that well-known school for otters and
other animal rotters, Bogwarts, who's motto was we
accept all animals warts and all, in fact let's go the
whole hog and say the more warts the better which
certainly made warthogs feel better I can tell you.

Continued over the page:

Bogwarts were proud to announce that after the latest round of BATS results it was officially the worst school for witchcraft and wizardry in the whole wizarding world.

The headmaster of Bogwarts was a wiley old badger wizard called Professor Bunglemore who had wizdom to spare, actually he didn't have any wizdom at all in fact he normally had the staff and pupils at Bogwarts tearing out their hair or holding their heads in their hands in despair, stinking the place out with his bad spells. Never more so than the day Professor Bunglemore picked up his wand instead of his baton then Repeated the spell *exsmellyarnos* and made the entire school orchestra disappear into thin air!

Bogwarts was situated by a river which was handy for the pupils as they could go home for lunch, get into fights, fly their kites and generally potter about to their hearts delight.

There was a magical babbling brook situated somewhere near the foreboding forest that pupils were never suppose to go anywhere near due to some terrible stories, although nobody quite new what these terrible stories were, although everybody agreed they were pretty terrible. (not unlike this one!)

Continued over the page:

The babbling brook was well know for babbling on and on and on which often kept pupils awake at night. Some of the animals could be heard to shout things Out like, 'will you keep that awful racket down we're trying to sleep here or if that babbling brook doesn't stop that awful hullabaloo soon we'll fill it in with a bag of quick drying cement otherwise we'll be forced to sleep in the foreboding forest in a luxury tent or go and rent a nice little flat somewhere in kent until the babbling brook repents.'

Which the babbling brook would reply ....
'I'm sorry but what do you expect I'm a babbling brook?
For heavens sake, its just second nature for me to babble you horrible rabble!'

The pupils who all lived along the river, which lay within a stone's throw from the grounds of Bogwarts were transported to and from the school by the Bogwarts Express, which was an old tractor and trailer driven by Baddrid the lovable clumsy giant. The Bogwarts express which was anything but, was exceedingly popular with pupils and teachers alike while at the same time being considered a little lame, which took so long to collect all the pupils and get them to Bogwarts that by the time they had arrived it was almost time to turn around and go home again,

Continued over the page:

which everybody at Bogwarts agreed was a terrible,
terrible shame although nobody did anything about all
the same.
Professor Bunglemore, a teacher of the old school who
liked the pupils of Bogwarts to read *Trixie Potter*
books as part of the curriculum,
which Harry and his pals thought a little uncool and
much preferred to read books by the author K.J.-
Howlins about wizards and witches and Goblins and
Giants and other such incomprehensible things.
Titles by K.J.Howlins included:
Garry Rotter and The Philosophical Argument.
Garry Rotter and the Sorcerers Dentist.
Garry Rotter and the True Blood Vampire Prince.
Garry Rotter and the Chambermaids secrets.
Garry Rotter and the Deadly Marshmallows.
Which was originally called the *Deadly Gallows* but the
Publishers Doomsbury reminded the author it was
suppose to be a children's book and so the title was
changed although K.J.Howlins was said to be furious at
the title change as she said the Deadly Gallows was a
far funnier title than the Deadly Marshmallows.
(Actually K.J.Howlins was cool like she always is.)
Other characters in this story to come in at a later date
Are Drake Malcontent an even bigger rotter than
Harry, a male swan hence the name Drake.

Continued over the page:

Harry's two best pals, Cora Blimey a wizard of an otter witch and Don "snotter" Sneezly another Wizard otter but nowhere near as big a rotter as Harry or Drake Malcontent, who had a couple of scurrilous pals of his own Scab and Boil who were recently expelled for their part in the robbery of Blingots and thrown down a wishing well, wishing they hadn't been expelled! There's also Professor Snake as thin as a rake and as slimey as any of the professors at Bogwarts who liked nothing more than putting Harry and his pals on report the spoilsport and to tell their parents they were always bottom of the class the vile viperous snake in the grass.

And later on in this tale there will be numerous mentions of the houses at Bogwarts.

Snivelling, Wiffindor, Balderdash and Piffle.

And how harry and his pals also nearly got themselves expelled for keeping live dragon's in the bogwarts cellar for their heated games of Dungeon & Dragons!

And of course Baddrid the clumsy giant who was trying To start his own pottery business as well as several mentions of the croak of invisibility and the thrilling Chase to find out if the philosopher's ringtone is in fact *I wish it could be Xmas Everyday* by Wizzard or not!

The rest of this story continues in the follow up book
A Hullabaloo at the local Zoo 2 , that's if I can put
down the Playstation long enough to finish it.
Which will be followed shortly by my first novel,

The Crystal Labyrinth Chronicles(Book One)
A book of the fantasy genre to jar your funny
bone but in a humours way. Jam packed full of
Witches, Wizards, Goblins, Boggards, Talking
Dragons, Bored Time Lords,
Seven Clawed Sporatours, Chivalrous Knights,
Chroniclers like Bartholomew Atticus Spoad
and Beezle T. Bodkin, Scurrilous Sorcerers like
Selivious Thiltskin, Guardians, Bugaboos,
Magicians like Theodore Shrimpkin and his
loyal trusty companion Kroll, A Troll of
considerable intelligence and standing within the
hamlet of Tarrin for his work for the council of
Corbayith. Book shops like The Books of
Antiquities Spells Potions and other
miscellaneous marvels,

Continued over the page:

383

a veritable cornucopia of delights run by the proprietor a one Morphious Wizenbaum III and his short sighted apprentice Zachariah Finklestein.

Changelings, Unicorns, Soothsayers and the Magical Kingdoms of Ffordaar and Yaltor.

A World in a parallel Universe where time literally runs backwards.

A tale which falls into the realms of fantasy from the very first word. A story which centres around the search for the long lost golden book of spells (which was so badly spelt only a few chroniclers could actually make head or tail of it), although actually it hadn't been lost but just mislayed by an absent minded librarian. A World that has two suns and thirteen moons. After spending time within the pages of this book all will become crystal clear, and if you believe that you really are living in a fantasy world!!

Continued over the page:

But for all that The Cyrystal Labyrinth Chronicles (Book One) is nothing if not a darn good old fashion yarn with I hasten to add the obligatory open ending for the continuation of the trilogy.

Actually having said all that my next book is called Goblins! and that isn't a fairytale! (lie)

I hope you enjoy my books and I hope it encourages
you to write your own poems, rhymes and stories.
But if you don't enjoy my books frankly I'm not that
bothered as long as you've paid for a copy and didn't
just take it out of the local library!

Don't forget there's nothing you can't do if you
Put your mind to it, as long as you put the work in.
And one final thing remember the real magic is inside
your own head. (Unless you're Frankenstein then it
might well be in somebody elses head!)

Michelle Sophie Gaynor & Pauline sorry I didn't have
enough room to include you at the beginning of the
book.
Anybody else I forgot will be included in ....
The Crystal Labyrinth Chronicles (Book One)
or Goblins!

Live Long & Prosper MaRk RoLAnD LaNgDaLe